IMPROVING TEACHING

The Analysis of Classroom Verbal Interaction

EDMUND AMIDON   Temple University

ELIZABETH HUNTER   Hunter College
of the City University
of New York

IMPROVING TEACHING

The Analysis of Classroom Verbal Interaction

HOLT, RINEHART AND WINSTON, INC.

New York   Chicago   San Francisco   Toronto   London

Cover photo courtesy of The New School for Social
Research

March, 1967

Copyright © 1966 by Holt, Rinehart and Winston, Inc.
Library of Congress Catalog Card Number: 66–24390

2561751
Printed in the United States of America

In writing this book we have been influenced by
many people in the field of professional education:
our students, our teachers, and our colleagues.
The major influence, however, has been the work of
Ned A. Flanders, and this book
is dedicated to him.

Preface

In recent years there has been a considerable amount of research in the area of teacher-pupil verbal interaction—classroom talk. Thus far, however, this research has not been readily available to the practitioner. This is one of the first texts to translate the knowledge gained from the research in classroom verbal interaction into usable, practical course material.

The authors describe teaching as an interactive process, primarily involving classroom talk, which takes place between teacher and pupils and occurs during certain definable activities. The teaching activities defined are motivating, planning, informing, leading discussion, disciplining, counseling, and evaluating. Each of these activities is discussed through a series of situations involving them, and, in addition, the classroom talk that has occurred is analyzed and categorized through a classification system called the Verbal Interaction Category System (VICS). The VICS categorizes classroom talk according to whether pupils or teachers are talking and according to whether the talk is initiatory or responsive. The VICS is presented in Chapter 2 and again in greater detail in the Appendix for those who want a more technical understanding of the use of the system through the construction and interpretation of matrices.

Thus, the VICS and the teaching activities (motivating, planning, informing, leading discussion, disciplining, counseling, and evaluating) are two separate and distinct entities, although both are used in this book to describe teaching. The VICS divides talk according to whether it consists of questions, acceptance of ideas or feelings, giving directions, and so forth, and the various talk categories are used to analyze the teaching activities. Therefore, this book presents situations that involve classroom talk during teaching activities and the VICS is utilized to analyze the teacher-pupil talk.

Each situation in this book is accompanied by an analysis and a skill session. The analyses examine the talk that takes place in the situations and the skill sessions give readers an opportunity to practice various kinds of verbal behavior so that they may be more capable of selecting appropriate verbal behavior for each of the various teaching activities. This book is constructed so that teaching is examined, analyzed, and practiced. In this way, the authors hope to enable readers to translate course work into classroom action.

Improving Teaching: The Analysis of Classroom Verbal Interaction is written for undergraduate and graduate methods courses and courses that focus upon the teaching process. The book is particularly valuable for use with student teachers and interns, as well as in-service teachers, since these groups are directly involved with pupils in the schools.

Philadelphia, Pennsylvania   E.A.
New York, New York   E.H.

July 1966

Contents

CHAPTER   5   Informing

CHAPTER   6   Leading Discussion

CHAPTER   7   Disciplining   128

IMPROVING TEACHING

The Analysis of Classroom Verbal Interaction

CHAPTER 1

Teaching

TEACHING DEFINED

Teaching is described in this book as an interactive process, primarily involving classroom talk, which takes place between teacher and pupils and occurs during certain definable activities. The teaching activities recognized here are: motivating, planning, informing, leading discussion, disciplining, counseling, and evaluating. Classroom talk can be classified and analyzed, and in this book it is categorized according to whether teacher or pupils are talking, and according to whether the talk is initiatory or responsive. The categories include: presenting information, giving direction, asking questions, accepting or rejecting responses, and silence. The teaching activities and the classroom talk categories are two separate and distinct entities, and both are used in this book to describe teaching.

Many educators recognize the importance of talk in teaching, and many consider teaching to be an interactive process. According to Flanders, "The chances are better than 60 percent that you will hear someone talking if you are in an elementary or secondary school classroom." [1] Meux and Smith write, "Teaching behavior is primarily verbal." [2] A committee of the American Educational Research Association calls teaching a "form of interpersonal influence aimed at changing the behavior potential of another person." [3] Marie Hughes defines teaching as "interaction used in its

---

[1] Ned A. Flanders, *Teacher Influence, Pupil Attitudes, and Achievement*, U.S. Department of Health, Education, and Welfare, Office of Education, Cooperative Research Monograph no. 12 (Washington, D.C.: U.S. Government Printing Office, 1965), p. 1.

[2] Milton Meux and B. Othanel Smith, "Logical Dimensions of Teaching Behavior," in B. J. Biddle and W. J. Ellena (eds.), *Contemporary Research on Teacher Effectiveness* (New York: Holt, Rinehart and Winston, Inc., 1964), p. 129.

[3] N. L. Gage (ed.), *Handbook of Research on Teaching* (Skokie, Ill.: Rand McNally & Company, 1963), p. 91.

dictionary sense of mutual or reciprocal action or influence." [4] And Stolurow and Pahel state that ". . . teaching is fundamentally a social process involving communication and interaction between at least two people, a teacher and a student. It is a kind of dialectic in which both serve as teacher and student at different times and at different levels. A teacher is not only instructing a student, but is also learning about that student, and using what he learns in making decisions about what to do next in the course of his teaching. Similarly, the student is not only learning, but he is providing information to the teacher, which in turn, guides the teacher in the ongoing interaction." [5]

IMPROVING TEACHING

There is general agreement among educators that teaching needs considerable improvement. Why, with all the effort put into the preparation of teachers, into the in-service education of teachers, and into teachers' individual efforts to modify and improve their work with youngsters, is not teaching far more effective than it is? Why do researchers engaged in classroom observation find that teachers are so controlling, restrictive and inhibiting? [6] Why is it that teachers tend to do most of the talking (about 70 percent in the average classroom, according to Flanders)? [7] Teachers would undoubtedly like to involve pupils more creatively in the teaching process, would like pupils to participate more, ask more imaginative and thoughtful questions, engage in more creative thinking. Why, then, do they tend to teach as they themselves were taught as youngsters, or as they see others teach in the schools, rather than in the ways they read about and talk about in professional education courses? Why is it true today, as it was in 1903 when John Dewey prepared this statement, that "The student adjusts his actual methods of teaching, not

---

4 Marie M. Hughes, "Utah Study of the Assessment of Teaching," in Arno A. Bellack (ed.), *Theory and Research in Teaching* (New York: Columbia University, Teachers College, Bureau of Publications, 1963), pp. 25–36.

5 L. Stolurow and K. Pahel, "Letter to the Editors," *Harvard Educational Review* (Summer, 1963), p. 384.

6 See Flanders; also Hughes, pp. 25–36; and Arno A. Bellack and others, *The Language of the Classroom: Meanings Communicated in High School Teaching*, U.S. Department of Health, Education, and Welfare, Office of Education, Cooperative Research Project no. 1497 (New York: Institute of Psychological Research, Columbia University, 1963).

7 Flanders, p. 1.

to the principles which he is acquiring, but to what he sees succeed and fail in an empirical way from moment to moment. . . . In this way the controlling habits of the teacher finally get fixed with comparatively little reference to principles in the psychology, logic, and history of education. In theory, these latter are dominant; in practice the moving forces are the devices and methods which are picked up through blind experimentation; through examples which are not rationalized; through precepts which are more or less arbitrary and mechanical; through advice based upon the experience of others." [8]

In 1929, Dewey suggested that so much in education was the result of "routine, tradition, accident and transitory accidental influences," [9] because the field lacked the "existence of systematic methods of inquiry, which when they are brought to bear on a range of facts, enable us to understand them better and to control them more intelligently, less haphazardly and with less routine." [10] He went on to suggest that education needed to rely less upon the intuition of practitioners and more upon the methods of science. This need is still present today.

In recent years, research (systematic methods of inquiry) has examined classroom verbal behavior—the *sine qua non* of teaching—and several systems for categorizing this behavior have been constructed as a result. This book presents, as a teaching tool, a system for analyzing classroom interaction called the Verbal Interaction Category System. This teaching tool is designed to help teachers move away from tradition and blind experimentation, in the words of Dewey, toward intelligent control of their verbal behavior. In other words, the Verbal Interaction Category System is designed to improve teaching.

It is axiomatic that the teacher is the most influential person in the classroom. Since talk is such a vital part of teaching, and since the teacher's verbal behavior directly influences pupils' verbal behavior, it follows that teacher talk is tremendously important in education. The authors believe that teachers and prospective teachers can learn to consciously control their verbal behavior in order to make their teaching *less* accidental, haphazard and routine—

---

8 John Dewey, "The Relation of Theory to Practice in Education," *National Society for the Scientific Study of Education*, Third Yearbook, 1904. Reprinted by the Association for Student Teaching, Bull. 17, 1962 (Cedar Falls, Iowa: State College of Iowa), p. 7.

9 John Dewey, "The Sources of a Science of Education," *Kappa Delta Pi Lecture Series* (New York: Liveright Publishing Corporation, 1929), p. 10.

10 Dewey, "The Relation of Theory to Practice in Education," p. 8.

in order to improve their teaching. The Verbal Interaction Category System is presented in this book to help teachers become less restrictive, controlling, and inhibiting, and more creative and releasing in their verbal behavior, and thus in their teaching. The Verbal Interaction Category System (VICS) is designed to help teachers select their verbal behavior so that their practice will be more in line with what they want it to be, so that, to paraphrase Dewey's title, there will be more of a relation between theory and practice in education.[11] The VICS will be discussed in detail in Chapter 2, and then will be used to analyze classroom discussion in situations which involve teachers and pupils in the various teaching activities. Readers will have an opportunity to analyze the classroom talk of other teachers, and also to practice regulating their own verbal behavior.

TEACHING ACTIVITIES

The classroom talk of teachers and pupils revolves around certain definable activities. These teaching activities or functions may be somewhat differently named, and they may also be divided up in varied ways. Sorenson and Husek name six teaching activities which they call role dimensions. Their six dimensions are: information giver, advisor, motivator, counselor, referrer and disciplinarian.[12] Raths identifies a number of teaching functions, of which the following seven would or could occur in the classroom as teachers work with pupils: explaining, informing or showing how; initiating, directing or administering; unifying the group; giving security; clarifying attitudes, beliefs and problems; diagnosing learning problems; and evaluating.[13]

In this book only those activities which directly involve the teacher with pupils will be identified and discussed, because teaching is defined here as an interactive process in which the teacher engages with pupils. Teachers participate in a wide variety of professional acts which do not directly involve them with pupils, such as planning outside the classroom for teaching, meeting with parents, joining in staff meetings and engaging in community affairs.

11 Dewey, "The Relation of Theory to Practice in Education," p. 8.
12 G. Sorenson and T. Husek, "Development of a Measure of Teacher Role Expectations," *American Psychologist*, vol. 18 (1963), p. 389. (Abstract)
13 Louis Raths, "What Is a Good Teacher?" *Childhood Education*, May, 1964, p. 451. Also no. 8602 in *Professional Reprints in Education* (Columbus, Ohio: Charles E. Merrill Books, Inc., 1965).

The teaching activities of motivating, planning, informing, leading discussion, disciplining, counseling, and evaluating have been introduced here as the seven teaching functions to be presented in this book. The next chapter will discuss the Verbal Interaction Category System, and describe the nature of the rest of the book.

CHAPTER 2

Analyzing Verbal Interaction in the Classroom

This chapter will introduce the Verbal Interaction Category System (VICS), a tool for analyzing classroom talk. Classroom talk is, of course, that verbal interaction which takes place between teacher and pupils and between pupils and pupils. The categories in the VICS, twelve in all, will be used to describe and analyze the talk in the classroom situations which are presented in this book.

The VICS is a system for studying the interactive verbal behavior of teacher and pupils in the classroom. Systems for such study are relatively recent in the field of education. Researchers have begun looking at the relationship between the verbal behavior of the teacher and such outcomes as pupil attitude and achievement; and a variety of systems designed to analyze teacher-pupil interaction in the classroom have been developed—one of the first by Anderson[1] in 1939. Others, developed by Withall,[2] Flanders,[3] Medley and Mitzel,[4] Hughes,[5] Smith,[6] Bellack,[7] Gallagher and Aschner[8] and Taba[9] are particularly well known.

1 H. H. Anderson, "The Measurement of Domination and of Socially Integrative Behavior in Teachers' Contacts With Children," *Child Development,* vol. 10 (1939), pp. 73–89.
2 John Withall, "The Development of a Technique for the Measurement of Social-Emotional Climate in Classrooms," *Journal of Experimental Education,* vol. 17 (1949), pp. 347–361.
3 Edmund J. Amidon and Ned A. Flanders, *The Role of the Teacher in the Classroom* (Minneapolis: Paul S. Amidon and Associates, 1963).
4 Donald M. Medley and Harold E. Mitzel, "A Technique for Measuring Classroom Behavior," *Journal of Educational Psychology,* vol. 49 (1958), pp. 86–92.
5 Marie M. Hughes, "Utah Study of the Assessment of Teaching," in Arno A. Bellack (ed.), *Theory and Research in Teaching* (New York: Columbia University, Teachers College, Bureau of Publications, 1963), pp. 25–36.

Many educators believe that systems for studying classroom verbal interaction hold great promise for the field of education. Studies seem to show that teachers are remarkably similar in their verbal behavior, and since the teacher is the most influential person in the classroom, the interaction patterns between teachers and pupils are also similar. Systems for analyzing classroom talk can tell us what actually occurs in classrooms, and they may also provide us with tools for preparing teachers who will be able to consciously select their verbal teaching patterns according to the goals they wish to achieve.

The VICS has been particularly developed as a tool for use in teacher education. It is designed to help teachers and prospective teachers become aware of the importance of verbal behavior in the classroom. The research of many educators indicates that the kind of verbal behavior in which the teacher engages has direct and immediate effect upon the verbal behavior of pupils. And verbal behavior—talk—is the major activity of teaching. "Of course, nonverbal communication does exist and is not unimportant . . . but occurs less frequently than verbal communication and the two are usually highly correlated. The frown is most often associated with statements that express disapproval, the smile with statements of approval." [10]

The Verbal Interaction Category System, then, is presented as a tool to be acquired by teachers and future teachers so that they may be released from the need to teach as they were taught, or to teach in the style of their cooperating teacher, or in a style which somehow emerges without their conscious consent. The

6 B. Othanel Smith, "A Conceptual Analysis of Instructional Behavior," *Journal of Teacher Education*, vol. 14, no. 3 (1963), pp. 294–298.

7 Arno A. Bellack and others, *The Language of the Classroom: Meanings Communicated in High School Teaching*, U.S. Department of Health, Education, and Welfare, Office of Education, Cooperative Research Project no. 1497 (New York: Institute of Psychological Research, Columbia University, 1963).

8 James J. Gallagher and Mary Jane M. Aschner, "A Preliminary Report: Analyses of Classroom Interaction," *Merrill-Palmer Quarterly of Behavior and Development*, vol. 9 (July, 1963), pp. 183–194.

9 Hilda Taba and others, *Thinking in Elementary School Children*, U.S. Department of Health, Education, and Welfare, Office of Education, Cooperative Research Project no. 1574 (San Francisco: San Francisco State College, 1964).

10 Ned A. Flanders, *Teacher Influence, Pupil Attitudes, and Achievement*, U.S. Department of Health, Education, and Welfare, Office of Education, Cooperative Research Monograph no. 12 (Washington, D.C.: U.S. Government Printing Office, 1965), p. 1.

VICS is not a confining system—not a "teaching by numbers" recipe. Rather it is designed to free teachers so that they may choose their verbal behavior according to what they wish to accomplish. The VICS is offered in the hope that it will liberate practitioners from teaching that is too often imitative or instinctual rather than thoughtful and original.

The reader should become familiar with the twelve categories of the VICS and the descriptions of them as they are presented in this chapter. For those who want to learn more about the system, and the way in which classroom conversation can be tallied and plotted on a matrix to present an objective picture of the verbal patterns of the classroom, a complete discussion of the system and its use is presented in the Appendix.

THE VERBAL INTERACTION CATEGORY SYSTEM

The Verbal Interaction Category System is based upon Flanders' work, and contains twelve categories for analyzing classroom verbal behavior. The accompanying table lists the categories in the VICS. The categories are grouped according to whether they involve teacher talk or pupil talk, and according to whether the talk is initiatory or responsive.

THE VICS CATEGORIES

Teacher-Initiated Talk

1. *Gives Information or Opinion* This category is used when the teacher is presenting facts or opinions to the class, either in the form of short statements or in the form of extended lecture. Generally, when the teacher is presenting content, this category is used. Explanation and orientation would fall in this category. During the interchange of discussion a teacher often gives information or opinion. Rhetorical questions such as, "We wouldn't expect that the government would have ceded power willingly, would we?" are included here.

2. *Gives Direction* When the teacher tells the students to take some specific action, this category is used. Examples of category 2 are: "Open

THE VERBAL INTERACTION CATEGORY SYSTEM (VICS)

Teacher-Initiated Talk	**1.** Gives Information or Opinion: presents content or own ideas, explains, orients, asks rhetorical questions. May be short statements or extended lecture.
	2. Gives Direction: tells pupil to take some specific action; gives orders; commands.
	3. Asks Narrow Question: asks drill questions, questions requiring one or two word replies or yes-or-no answers; questions to which the specific nature of the response can be predicted.
	4. Asks Broad Question: asks relatively open-ended questions which call for unpredictable responses; questions which are thought-provoking. Apt to elicit a longer response than 3.
Teacher Response	**5.** Accepts: (5a) Ideas: reflects, clarifies, encourages or praises ideas of pupils. Summarizes, or comments without rejection.
	(5b) Behavior: responds in ways which commend or encourage pupil behavior.
	(5c) Feeling: responds in ways which reflect or encourage expression of pupil feeling.
	6. Rejects: (6a) Ideas: criticizes, ignores or discourages pupil ideas.
	(6b) Behavior: discourages or criticizes pupil behavior. Designed to stop undesirable behavior. May be stated in question form, but differentiated from category 3 or 4, and from category 2, Gives Direction, by tone of voice and resultant effect on pupils.
	(6c) Feeling: ignores, discourages or rejects pupil expression of feeling.
Pupil Response	**7.** Responds (7a) Predictably: relatively short replies, usually, which follow category 3. May also follow category 2, i.e. "David, you may read next."
to Teacher:	(7b) Unpredictably: replies which usually follow category 4.
	8. Responds to Another Pupil: replies occurring in conversation between pupils.
Pupil-Initiated Talk	**9.** Initiates Talk to Teacher: statements which pupils direct to teacher without solicitation from teacher.
	10. Initiates Talk to Another Pupil: statements which pupils direct to another pupil which are not solicited.
Other	**11.** Silence: pauses or short periods of silence during a time of classroom conversation.
	Z. Confusion: considerable noise which disrupts planned activities. This category may accompany other categories or may totally preclude the use of other categories.

your books to page 5," "Take your seats now," and "Add the following numbers as quickly as possible." Directions may be given in question form, as for example, "Will everyone turn around now?" or "Can
you come here for a moment, Jane?"

3. *Asks Narrow Question*   If the specific nature of the response can
be predicted, then this category is used. Drill questions and questions
requiring one word or yes-or-no answers fall into this category. "How
much is 3 and 3?" "What is the capital of France?" "Is that correct?"
"What happened next in the story?" "What are the principal exports
of Brazil?" and "Did you like that plan?" are examples of narrow
questions.

4. *Asks Broad Question*   Questions that fall into this category would
be relatively open-ended; the kind that call for unpredictable responses. When the teacher asks questions that are thought-provoking,
that require reasoning or extended expression of opinion or feeling,
this category is used. The broad question is apt to elicit longer responses than the narrow question. Examples of broad questions are:
"Can you tell me some things you know about the number '3'?" "What
are some reasons that Paris came to be the capital of France?" "What
are some other things the author might have written next in this
story?" "What are some ways in which the history and geography of
Brazil might influence its production and exports?" "What do you
think about that plan?" and "How do you feel about what she said?"

Teacher Response

5a. *Accepts Ideas*   When the teacher reflects, clarifies, encourages or
praises an idea of a pupil, then this category is used. If the teacher
summarizes the ideas of a pupil or of several pupils, comments upon
the ideas without rejecting them or simply reflects them by restatement, this category is indicated. Saying "Yes," "Good," "That's an
interesting idea," and "So you think the governor acted wisely," are
examples of category 5a.

5b. *Accepts Behavior*   Responses to pupil behavior which encourage
or praise that behavior fall into this category. Such statements as,
"The boys and girls in this group are cooperating well," "Billy knows
how to use books properly," "You told that story with marvelous expression," "That's a colorful picture," "You can be proud of the way

you behaved on our trip," and "Good work," are examples of accept-ance of behavior.

5c. *Accepts Feeling* When the teacher responds to pupil feeling in an accepting manner or merely reflects their feelings, this category is used. "I know that it's a warm day and many of us would rather be outside," "Of course you feel disappointed because there isn't any as-sembly program today," "I'd be happy, too, if that happened to me," "No wonder you're crying," and "You're very angry," are examples of category 5c.

6a. *Rejects Ideas* This category is used when the teacher criticizes, ignores or discourages pupil ideas. "Can someone else tell us the right answer?" "That's not right," "Where did you ever get *that* idea!" "Is that what I asked you to discuss?" and "New York is not one of the New England States" are examples of rejection. Notice that some of these examples were stated in question form, but would be taken by the pupils as criticism, and are clearly rejection of ideas.

6b. *Rejects Behavior* Teacher comments that are designed to dis-courage or criticize pupil behavior fall into this category. "I said to sit down!" "We shouldn't have our books open now," "Where do you think you are?" "Stop that at once," and "Never give me a paper like that again," are all expressions of rejection of behavior. Some of these examples may appear to fall into the category of questions or direc-tions. The tone of voice, the resultant effect upon pupils, and the fact that they are designed to *stop* behaviors which the teacher con-siders to be *undesirable* are what cause them to be categorized as teacher comments which reject pupil behavior.

6c. *Rejects Feeling* When teachers respond to expressions of pupil feeling by discouraging or criticizing them, then the category of re-jecting feeling is being used. "Aren't you ashamed of yourself for crying?" "Just because there's no assembly today is no reason to mope," "There's no need to bring our personal feelings up," and "There's absolutely no reason for you to be worried," are examples of this category.

Pupil Response

7a. *Responds to Teacher Predictably* This response would ordi-narily follow category 3, a narrow or predictable response question from the teacher, and would tend to be a relatively short reply. Category 7a may also follow category 2, Gives Direction, as when the teacher says, "David, read the sentence at the top of the page." A response that is incorrect may still be considered to be in this category.

7b. *Responds to Teacher Unpredictably* This category would usually follow the asking of a broad or unpredictable response question by the teacher. However, it is possible for a pupil to give an unpredictable response to a question which is categorized as narrow. For instance, when a teacher asks, "What was the cause of this conflict?" a pupil might reply, "It seems to me that there wasn't any one cause. I think there were many factors at work." This kind of response, however, is rarely found in the classroom. It would be more likely that an unpredictable response to a narrow question would be an irrelevant response, as when the teacher asks, "How many of you had milk for breakfast this morning?" and a pupil responds, "Last night we had ice cream for dessert."

8. *Responds to Another Pupil* Whenever one pupil responds to the question or statement of another pupil, this category is being used. When there is conversation between pupils, the replies are examples of category 8.

Pupil-Initiated Talk

9. *Talks to Teacher* If a pupil initiates a conversation with the teacher, then category 9 is used. "Will we have art today?" "I don't understand how to do this problem," "Here's a clipping I brought in for our social studies project," "Would you repeat that last part again?" are all examples of category 9.

10. *Talks to Another Pupil* Any conversation which one pupil initiates with another pupil falls into this category.

Other

11. *Silence* Category 11 occurs whenever there are pauses or periods of silence during a time of classroom talk. Long periods of silence, for instance, when the class is engaged in seat work or silent reading, are of a different nature because these silences are not really a part of verbal interaction.

Z. *Confusion* When there is considerable noise which disrupts planned activities, this category is used.

USING THIS BOOK

The next seven chapters will each deal with one of the teaching activities defined in Chapter 1. After a brief further discussion of the specific teaching activity, a number of situations involving pupils and teachers as they engage in that particular activity will be presented. After each situation there is an analysis, when the talk or part of the talk is discussed using the VICS. Often the reader is asked to analyze the talk, which means that he should become familiar with the VICS categories as they are presented in this chapter. The categories will, however, be further defined and discussed in the various analyses of the situations.

In addition to the analysis, there is a skill session following each situation. In these skill sessions the reader is encouraged to practice various kinds of teaching behavior in order that he may be more capable of selecting the kind he wants to use as he engages, in reality, in the various teaching activities. A verbal behavior must be in one's repertoire if one is to have the option of deciding upon its use. The student teacher and the regular teacher will also be able to try out the skill session activities with their pupils in school. And, in addition to the conscious use of language during skill sessions, each class group using this book will probably want to practice its verbal behavior skills during the entire range of the education course in which this book is being used.

Some of the skill sessions in this book call for role playing. During role-playing sessions the college instructor may occasionally play the part of the classroom teacher, but ordinarily the students themselves will try out the teacher roles. While role playing may at first seem stilted and unnatural, the group will become accustomed to this kind of activity, and will have meaningful opportunities to try on various teaching behaviors. Class members will also have opportunities to see what it is like to be a pupil. During role playing, it is important for the participants to actually take the parts assigned, and not merely talk *about* what such a person might or would say. In a sense, role playing is an attempt to temporarily *become* someone else. Following the role playing sessions it is appropriate to discuss the feelings of the participants, as well as the techniques which have been used. The authors believe that role playing is one of the most important means available for teachers and prospective teachers to broaden their teaching repertoire.

To learn to teach well it is apparently not enough to have a knowledge of subject matter, a knowledge of curriculum materials and organization, a knowledge of the philosophy and history of education, a knowledge of educational psychology and child development, an understanding of social issues and a chance to practice teaching under the guidance of a supervising teacher. Nor will the picture change if we add liking children and having a strong desire to teach. What *is* essential, in addition, is for every teacher and prospective teacher to become engaged in the study of teaching and in the acquisition of skill in the genuine "how" of teaching, that is, skill in the interactive talk which occurs during teaching activities. By analyzing, studying, and practicing behavior through the conscious selection and examination of verbal interaction during the various teaching activities, one can acquire teaching skill. This book has been written so that teaching behavior will be examined, analyzed, and then, tried on.

CHAPTER 3

Motivating

Although motivating activity is often thought of as occurring at the start of a new lesson or unit, teachers engage in this activity to some degree throughout their teaching—with more or less success, depending upon their teaching behavior. An interesting introduction to a topic without the follow-through necessary to sustain the attention of youngsters will not accomplish the teacher's intended aim, which is to engage pupils for the duration of the topic, whether it involves a single lesson or an extended unit.

Teachers may engage in motivating activity in ways that create and sustain interest in youngsters; in ways that build upon already existing interests; in ways that bring about a certain behavioral compliance without arousing either interest or dislike; in ways that cause pupils to lose whatever natural or initial interest they may have had; or in ways that not only fail to arouse interest or evoke disinterest, but actually cause pupils to dislike certain topics, subjects, and even schooling in general. To illustrate the possibilities just listed, we can point out that a teacher may help children who have never had much interest in books or reading become avid and discriminating readers; he may help pupils who already like to read, widen their interest and find new delight in books; he may see to it that children read and report on a certain number of assigned books without either helping them to extend their out-of-school reading or causing them to actively dislike books; he may teach in such a way that pupils lose their former interest in reading; or he may not only be unable to interest pupils in reading, but may unwittingly be the cause of preventing children from learning to read at all and may also cause them to believe that books are irrelevant to their lives and that school is a place where one is made to feel inadequate.

Teachers may attempt to motivate pupils in a wide variety of ways. For instance, they may use the promise of reward or the threat of punishment. These methods may succeed with some pupils and fail with others. One has only to think of the pupils who never receive the offered reward of a good grade, or a gold star, or a chance to be class monitor, to know that rewards often are not successful. And anyone who has watched the same youngsters stay after school year after year for not behaving as the teacher wishes, or not accomplishing what the teacher expects, will know that punishment is often an unsuccessful motivating device.

Ideally, children should be motivated to learn because *they* want to find out more than *they* already know, because *they* want to improve *their* skills—be these skills social, emotional or cognitive. Children are naturally curious, but sometimes teachers, without meaning to, stifle the interest of their pupils because of the way in which they teach. Of course, some pupils are much easier to motivate than others, because of a variety of factors including past school experiences. With pupils whose former school experiences have led them to expect failure, and whose curiosity has been somewhat dimmed by past repressions or simply by past pedagogical disinterest, the teacher's task can be difficult, because he must not only reawaken interest, but he must also modify attitudes by providing these youngsters with an honest sense of accomplishment within the school setting.

In this chapter the reader will find that the VICS category of asking questions is discussed rather fully in some of the analyses and skill sessions. This does not mean that questions are necessarily the best means for motivating pupils—just as the verbal category "giving information or opinion" need not be the primary or most useful verbal behavior for the teaching activity "informing." Probably a variety of verbal behaviors are appropriate for each teaching activity, although some may occur more than others at certain times. Which talk categories are used depends upon the requirements of the situation, the subject matter being covered, the make-up of the class, the personality of the teacher, and so forth.

No teacher would consciously want to inhibit the learning of youngsters. The situations which follow, and their accompanying analyses and skill sessions, are designed to help the reader examine various ways in which teachers motivate pupils and also to help improve motivating skills.

Situation 1A

Mrs. Arnold found that her kindergarten children frequently forgot their weekly milk money, and since she didn't like to see anyone go without milk she spent a considerable amount of time asking other teachers if they had extra cartons of milk and supplying cups so that the children could share with each other. Now that spring was here and fewer children were absent, the milk shortage was becoming acute. Mrs. Arnold decided that the children needed a talking-to.

"You all know, children," she began, "that Monday morning is when we collect milk money. But many of you are forgetting your money, and even though everyone has been good about sharing, and we can sometimes get extra milk from some of the other classes, there isn't always enough to go around. Now I've been thinking about this, and I've decided that beginning next week, anyone who doesn't bring in his money will just have to go without milk. We aren't going to have any more sharing, and we aren't going to ask other classes for extras. Perhaps then we'll be able to remember to bring our money in on Monday mornings. Do you think that's a good idea?"

"Yes," "Um hm," "The kids who don't remember money shouldn't have milk," and a general nodding of heads was the result.

"All right then," Mrs. Arnold said, "we're agreed on that. No money—no milk. Now, it's time to go outdoors. I'm looking for a nice quiet table ready to get sweaters."

ANALYSIS   The teacher in this case attempts to motivate her class to remember their milk money by telling them that in the future there will be no milk for children who forget their money. After presenting her opinion to the class she asks a narrow question, "Do you think that's a good idea?" and receives the support for her idea which she undoubtedly expected. Frequently children will not disagree with the suggestions of the teacher. However, verbal agreement does not mean that children will behave as the teacher suggests.

What do you think of this teacher's plan for motivating children to remember their milk money? What other things might this teacher do to help the children remember?

SKILL SESSION   "Do you think that's a good idea?" is an example of a narrow question which might be answered by the words "yes," "no," "maybe," or "I don't know." It may be broadened by rephrasing it, or modifying it. For example, one might say, "What do you think of this idea?" or "Is there any other way besides this that *you* can think of?" After stating an opinion or idea a teacher might say, "I can think of some reasons why this might not be such a good idea. What do you think some of these reasons are?"

Practice turning these narrow questions, which call for expression of opinion, into broad questions:

1. Do you like that solution?

2. Which is a better way to do this—Johnny's way or Billy's?

3. Does everybody agree?

4. Isn't that a good idea?

Situation 1B

Mrs. Pickett decided to talk with the children about the fact that so many of them were forgetting their milk money on Monday mornings. Now that spring was here and not so many children were absent, there was frequently a shortage of extra milk for distribution to those who had forgotten to bring money.

"Children," began Mrs. Pickett, "we have a problem which we need to discuss. Quite a few of you are forgetting to bring in milk money, and there's beginning to be a shortage of milk. What are some suggestions that might help us remember to bring in our money?"

The children had a number of responses.

"I think the kids who don't bring in money shouldn't have milk."

"I never bring in money 'cause I don't like milk and my mommy said I don't have to drink it."

"I wish we could have chocolate milk."

"My mother never remembers to remind me."

"Billy always spills his milk, and he never even finishes it."

"I try to remember, but sometimes I keep forgetting."

"Well, now," Mrs. Pickett said, "let's see what suggestions we have so far. Some children just seem to have trouble remembering, and even mothers might have trouble about remembering. We always try to share our milk, but someone has suggested that maybe the children who don't remember their money should just not get any milk. The school says that we can't order chocolate milk; and we have agreed that children who don't want milk don't have to drink it. What do you think about the idea of having the children who forget their money go without milk?"

"I think that's good."

"If they can't remember, too bad."

"Yeah, my mother don't forget."

"Well it ain't my fault if I forget."

"Me neither—it's not fair."

"Perhaps before we try taking the milk away," Mrs. Pickett suggested, "we ought to try to think of some other ways to help us remember better. Anybody have any ideas about that?"

"You could tell us to remember."

"She already tells us and we forget."

"You should tell our mothers so they'll give us the money."

"You could write the mothers a note and tell them to remember."

"That seems like a good idea," agreed Mrs. Pickett. "I can write notes to send home with you on Friday to remind your mothers about the money for Monday morning. We'll try that for the next week or so, and if that doesn't work we'll have to talk about this again. All right, now it's time for going outdoors. Table one, let's see if you can get your things from the coatroom so carefully that you don't knock anyone else's sweater from its hook."

ANALYSIS This teacher attempts to motivate her class to remember milk money by beginning with a broad question, "What are some suggestions that might help us remember to bring in our money?" She then accepts and summarizes several of the ideas expressed by the children and focuses the discussion of the class by asking a second question, slightly narrower than the first, "What do you think about the idea of having the children who forget their money go without milk?" After several responses, she expresses an opinion, "Perhaps before we try taking the milk away, we ought to try to think of some other ways to help us remember better," and then she asks a broad question, "Anybody have any ideas about that?" She then accepts and builds on a suggestion about writing the mothers a note as a reminder.

Mrs. Pickett, the teacher in this situation, gives the children an opportunity to participate in finding a solution to the milk money problem. What do you think of her method of motivating children as compared to the method of the teacher in situation 1A? Identify other things in their teaching which these two teachers seem to consider to be important, in addition to the immediate problem of having children remember to bring in their milk money.

SKILL SESSION   In one statement accept and summarize all seven of the following pupil remarks in a discussion of the importance of taking turns at the painting easel:

1. I never have a turn.
2. Nobody should make more than two paintings.
3. I don't like to paint. I'd rather play in the blocks.
4. Why can't we have two easels like Mrs. Brown?
5. I like to paint.
6. We should pick somebody to be after us.
7. You should tell the kids who can paint every day.

Situation 2

"Yesterday we had to go over these words again and again," said Miss Holmes to her first grade class. "Sometimes I think that this class will never learn. We spent half an hour on this lesson, but you children simply do not listen! You don't pay attention and you don't try. Now today we're going to go over the whole list again, and we're going to stay with it until you know every word. So sit up straight, feet flat on the floor and faces front. You are going to learn these words once and for all. Children who can't read don't go on to second grade, you know!"

ANALYSIS   Miss Holmes criticizes her class by rejecting their work and their behavior, and suggests that if their work doesn't improve they will not be promoted. Since criticism and rejection have unpredictable results at best, and may even accomplish the opposite effect to that which the teacher intends, what do you think might be the results of this teacher's behavior? What might be some alternative means of motivating these children to learn new words?

Miss Holmes' first statement, "Yesterday

we had to go over these words again and again," can be changed
from a rejecting statement to an informing statement by rephrasing
it in the following way: "We had some trouble with the words we
tried to learn yesterday, so we'll go over them again today." If the
phrase, "even though we worked hard" is added after "words we
tried to learn yesterday," then the statement includes acceptance of
behavior. Note that changing statements of rejection does not mean
that they necessarily must become statements of acceptance.

SKILL SESSION How can each of the following statements be
changed so that rejection of pupil behavior and ideas is eliminated:

1. Sometimes I think that this class will never learn.
2. We spent half an hour on this lesson, but you children simply
   do not listen!
3. You don't pay attention and you don't try.
4. You are going to learn these words once and for all.
5. Children who can't read don't go on to second grade, you know!

Situation 3

The third grade curriculum called for a
unit of study about the seasons and weather, including causes for the
variation in length of days and changes in temperature through the
year. Miss Harrington decided to start the unit on the first day of
spring by awakening the children's curiosity about some of the things
they would be studying for the next few weeks. For homework on the
last day of winter she asked the children to find out what would be
special about the next day.

The next day, she began by saying, "Remember yesterday I asked
you to find out what special day today would be? Some of you probably already knew, but you were very good about holding your information until today. Now . . . what is special about today?"

"The first day of spring," came a chorus of responses from the
children.

"Yes—today is the first day of a new season. Jack, can you tell us
the names of the seasons of the year, and perhaps one brief thing about
each?"

"Well," replied Jack, "there's winter, spring, summer, and fall. In winter it's cold, in summer it's hot, in fall it's—um. . . ."

"Let's not raise our hands unless we're specifically asked to during this discussion," Miss Harrington admonished the children whose hands noisily shot up as Jack hesitated. "You know it's annoying when you're trying to think and everyone starts waving hands in the air. Jack, can you tell us something about the leaves on the trees in the other two seasons?"

"Well—in the fall the leaves turn color and fall down, and in the spring the new leaves come out," Jack finished.

"So there are four seasons, and each is somewhat different from the others. During the next few weeks we're going to be studying about the seasons, and today I thought it might be a good idea to get out some questions—some of the things we would like to learn about. I have a question for us to start off with, and I'm going to put it up here on the board. My question is, 'Why isn't the first day of spring always a nice warm day?' You know, it's very cold out today. But we usually think of springtime as being a rather warm time, don't we?"

"Well, it's only the beginning of spring. Later on—in April, maybe—the days will be warmer," responded Karen.

"All right. Karen says it's only the very beginning of spring, and that's why it's still cold. Instead of trying to answer our questions today, let's just concentrate on getting out the questions, and we won't even try to think of answers—or at least, we won't tell our answers yet. Who has some question he'd like answered during this study?"

There was a pause. Then someone said, "I'd like to know why the first day of summer isn't always warm." Another child added, "I'd like to know why the first day of winter isn't always cold."

"Those questions are both related to the one we have up here on the board, aren't they? We might add a broader question that would cover all of these—something like, 'Why isn't every day in a season alike?' But perhaps we need to think a bit more about what happens during the year so that we can get some other questions out. Think about the length of time you have to play outside after school. Is there anything different about the hour you have to come into the house now from when you came in back about Christmas time?"

"Yes! It gets dark later, so we can stay out later."

"Oh—I have a question. I wonder why it gets dark earlier in the winter and later in the summer."

"And I have a question, too. Why is it colder in the winter than in the summer? Maybe it's because the sun doesn't shine for so long."

"Good questions. I'm getting these down on the board," said Miss Harrington.

"Remember we read in that Eskimo story that the sun doesn't set for a long time near the North Pole. Let's find out about that."

"My father has a clock that shows what time it is in different parts of the world. Maybe I could find out more about that and tell about it."

"Let's read over the questions that we have so far," suggested Miss Harrington as she finished writing on the board. "Barbara, will you start?"

QUESTIONS WE WANT TO ANSWER

1. Why isn't the first day of spring always a nice warm day?
2. Why isn't every day in a season alike?
3. Why does it get dark earlier in the winter than in the summer?
4. Why is it colder in the winter than in the summer?

"Good clear reading, Barbara. David, will you continue?" asked Miss Harrington.

5. Why doesn't the sun set for a long time in the North Pole?
6. Why do different parts of the world have different times on the same day?

"Well, we've certainly made a good beginning here," Miss Harrington told the class. "I know that many of you already have information about some of these things, but we'll have to wait until tomorrow to go on with this. Tomorrow we can get out some possible answers, and perhaps we'll find that we have many more questions. Sometime before the day is over, would you, Jill, copy the questions on this ditto sheet, and then we can run them off for everyone to have before we go home. Naturally we won't have all of the answers tomorrow, but we'll get started—and remember, every possible answer is acceptable in the beginning. As we go along we'll have to check on whether we're right or not. What are some of the ways we can find the answers to our questions . . . ?"

ANALYSIS   Miss Harrington attempts to motivate her class by involving them in planning the direction which their study will take. She asks broad questions such as "What are some of the things we would like to learn about?" and narrow questions such as "What is special about today?" She accepts all the children's ideas, but rejects some behavior.

When Jack hesitates in his response to her question and other class members jump in with noisily raised hands, Miss Harrington rejects their behavior with an explanation, and then asks Jack a narrow question which she is certain he can answer.

Since Miss Harrington is free to interject questions and suggestions at any time during the discussion, she might have held her initial sample question, "Why isn't the first day of spring always a nice warm day?" in order to leave the direction of the children's responses completely open. However, when the children merely rephrase her question, Miss Harrington accepts these repetitions and builds them into another question, "Why isn't every day in a season alike?" She then gives the class some information in order to change the direction of the children's questions.

If involvement in planning increases children's motivations for learning, then this class would seem to be well motivated to discover the answers to the questions raised.

SKILL SESSION Gallagher and Aschner have developed a system containing four categories that are particularly useful for thinking about questions.[1] The four categories are: cognitive memory, convergent, divergent, and evaluative. A discussion of these categories and some examples of each follow. From time to time you will be asked to modify questions or statements according to these categories.

Cognitive Memory Questions These questions call for facts or other items which can be recalled. A cognitive memory question is a narrow question and involves rote memory. Some examples are:

1. What is the largest city in New York State?
2. How did you come to school this morning?
3. Who remembers the name of this picture?
4. Name the ABC countries of South America.

Convergent Questions which call for "the analysis and integration of given or remembered data"[2] are convergent questions. Problem solving and reasoning are often involved in this category. The answers

1 James J. Gallagher and Mary Jane Aschner, "A Preliminary Report on Analyses of Classroom Interaction," *The Merrill-Palmer Quarterly of Behavior and Development*, vol. 9, no. 3 (1963).

2 Gallagher and Aschner, p. 187.

to these questions may be predictable, but convergent questions are always broader than cognitive memory questions. Whether they are categorized as broad or narrow questions according to the VICS depends on how predictable the responses are. Often, you need to know the background of the pupils in order to determine whether questions ask for reasoning or recall. Some examples of convergent questions are:

1. What is there about the position of New York City that accounts for its importance?
2. Suppose that overnight the school were picked up and moved four blocks away, and you were not told of the move. How could you go about finding it?
3. In what ways is *this* picture like *that* one?
4. Why are the ABC countries important in South America?

Divergent Questions   Questions in this category call for answers which are creative and imaginative; which move into new directions. Here are some divergent questions:

1. How might the lives of the people in New York City be different if the city were located in the torrid zone?
2. Invent some ways for coming to school which haven't yet been invented.
3. If our society put an extremely high value on art, and wanted to encourage as many people as possible to be artists, how would our schools be different and how would your after-school lives be different?
4. In what ways might Argentina, Brazil, and Chile be different if they had been colonized by England?

Evaluative Questions   These questions deal with "matters of judgment, value and choice." [3] They may be either broad or narrow. "Did you like that story?" is a narrow question; "How did you feel about that story?" is a broad question. Some examples of evaluative questions are:

1. Why would you like to live in New York City? Would you like to live in New York City?
2. What method of transportation would *you* like to use to come to school?

3 Gallagher and Aschner, p. 188.

3. What do you think about this picture? Do you like this picture?
4. What things would you particularly like to visit in Argentina? Would you prefer to be a cowboy *or* a gaucho?

The work of Gallagher and Aschner indicates that the kinds of questions which teachers ask evoke similar kinds of responses. That is, divergent questions cause pupils to engage in divergent thinking, and cognitive memory questions evoke cognitive memory responses.

"Can you tell us the names of the seasons of the year?" is an example of a cognitive memory question. To modify this in order to make it convergent, we might ask, "How are the seasons of the year alike, and how are they different?" Expressed divergently, the question could be phrased, "How would our way of life change if we had only one season?" And an example of an evaluative question on this topic would be, "Do you think it would be better to live in a climate which had a very long winter or a very long summer?"

Using the Gallagher and Aschner categories, modify these convergent questions so that you construct questions which are cognitive memory, divergent, and evaluative:

1. Why isn't the first day of spring always a nice warm day?
2. Why isn't every day in a season alike?
3. Why does it get dark earlier in the winter than in the summer?
4. Why is it colder in the winter than in the summer?
5. Why doesn't the sun set for a long time in the North Pole?
6. Why do different parts of the world have different times on the same day?

Situation 4A

Mr. Manero felt that the penmanship skills of his fourth grade class needed improvement. At times the class was a bit careless about legibility. "You know, boys and girls," he told them, "your mothers and fathers will be coming to school next week for Parents' Night, and I'm sure that they'll look forward to seeing samples of your work around the room. It would be nice to have one story or poem or article from each person displayed about the room.

You'll want to have your best handwriting on these papers so that your parents will be able to read them. I'm going to leave the choice to you as to what you would like to display. Get out your folders and look through them, and select one thing which you want to put up. Then take a piece of the good composition paper and begin making as fine a copy as you can. If you have any problems in deciding what to select, raise your hand and I'll come around."

ANALYSIS   Mr. Manero gives information and direction to the class in an attempt to motivate them to improve their handwriting. The children may be motivated to work carefully and well because of their desire to display good work for their parents. What do you think will be the long-term effect of this motivational technique on their handwriting?

The analysis and skill session which follow situation 4B are related to this situation.

Situation 4B

Mr. Boyd was concerned about the penmanship of his fourth grade class and felt that their skills needed improvement. "I have put this paragraph from your social studies book on the board, boys and girls," he told them, "and I want you to copy it in your very best handwriting. I'm going to go over your papers very carefully and those who have the best papers will receive gold stars. Anybody who receives three gold stars this week will have one of his papers put up on the bulletin board. So you will want to do your very best work. Now get started, and work very carefully."

ANALYSIS   Mr. Boyd gives information and direction to his class in an attempt to motivate them to improve their handwriting skills. He offers the reward of gold stars, introducing the element of competition. The children who are initially successful in earning gold stars may well continue to try for them, but what will happen to those children who do not earn stars? What do you think will be the carryover into the children's other handwriting efforts of this teacher's motivational techniques?

The teachers in situations 4A and 4B both give information and direction to their classes. In neither case are the children involved in discussion but in both cases opportunity for display is offered. In one case each pupil will have his work displayed, and in the other only the "best" work will be shown.

Both teachers give reasons for the need to write well. Mr. Boyd's reasons are that *he* wants the children to use their best handwriting, and that they will have a chance to earn a gold star as a reward. Mr. Manero's reason is that the children's parents will want to see good work.

Marie Hughes discusses the teacher's use of what she calls "public criteria" in giving the teacher's authority a less personal cast.[4] For instance, instead of saying, "I told you to get quiet," the teacher might say, "When we are this noisy we disturb the class next door." In Hughes' study of teaching behavior, she found that teachers tended to be very controlling in their actions, and often gave no reasons for the demands they put upon children.[5] She points out that reprimands are more just when explanations are made clear through public criteria, and that this might "aid in reducing the conflicts with authority." [6] Some of her examples of the use of public criteria are, "We had trouble with a certain kind of problem yesterday; therefore we will work on similar problems today," and "You have too many erasures on your paper to read it easily," instead of "I won't take a paper that looks like that." [7]

Do either of the teachers in situations 4A or 4B use public criteria in their attempts to motivate their pupils?

SKILL SESSION   When a teacher says, "Your noisy behavior is not making me very proud of you," he is not using public criteria. To use public criteria, one would have to phrase that sentence differently, saying, for instance, "Your noisy behavior is preventing other pupils from hearing this story."

Identify those statements in the following list which use public criteria:

1. Your work is good.

2. Your work is good because you have shown how you arrived at your answer.

---

4 Marie M. Hughes, "What Is Teaching? One Viewpoint," *Educational Leadership,* January, 1962, pp. 251–259.
5 *Ibid.,* p. 256.
6 *Ibid.*
7 *Ibid.*

3. Your work is good. It's just what I wanted.

4. Your work is good. It's much better than last time.

5. Your work is good, because you have such clear examples of action words.

6. If you are able to do all of the steps to this problem correctly,

   a. you'll make me very happy.

   b. we'll have a longer recess.

   c. you'll be able to do any new problems of this type on your own.

   d. you'll be able to check your own answers with good understanding.

Situation 5

Mrs. Delacorte began a study of the American Revolutionary War with her fifth grade class by giving them a brief quiz.

"I'm handing out this paper," Mrs. Delacorte told the class, "so that you can write down some information. These papers won't be graded, so don't think of this as a test in the usual sense, but please write legibly because I am going to collect your papers and read them. Then you'll get them back to keep. Do as well as you can because we're going to use these papers as a starting place for our discussions in social studies over the next few days. It will be interesting for you to compare your answers now with those you give after our study of the American Revolution—because that's our next topic. Here are the questions. I'll write them on the board."

1. Against what country did America fight in the Revolutionary War?

2. List two or three reasons why the revolution was fought.

3. What is a revolution?

"And, for homework, I'm going to put up one more question. Don't answer this in writing—just be prepared to discuss it tomorrow."

4. What things might be different in our country now if America had lost the revolution?

ANALYSIS Mrs. Delacorte is attempting to motivate her class by asking questions, broad and narrow, about a forthcoming unit of study.

Why is she careful to assure the children that these questions are not a test in the usual sense? What do you think of this method as a motivational technique? Would writing the answers to the questions have different motivational effects than discussing the answers?

SKILL SESSION   Using Gallagher and Aschner's system for categorizing questions (see Chapter 3, situation 3) modify each of the following questions so that they will elicit divergent responses:

1. Against what country did America fight in the Revolutionary War?
2. List two or three reasons why the revolution was fought.
3. What is a revolution?

Situation 6

The sixth grade class was scheduled to study Mexico next in social studies. Mr. Mitchell had prepared a bulletin board with colorful pictures from his files, had put out a number of books on Mexico, and had also arranged Mexican objects along the library shelves and the window sills.

When it was time for social studies period, Mr. Mitchell began by saying, "Some of you have already guessed from the things around the room that we're going to be studying Mexico now that we've finished with Canada. And I want to tell you again that I think you did a splendid job on Canada. The final reports were interesting and well prepared, and I think the groups really managed to hold our attention. The questions from the class were particularly thoughtful, and the committees did a good job of answering them. I would like to go about the study of Mexico in much the same way that we did Canada, and compare them, perhaps as a final project, perhaps as we go along. We'll see about that later. Who can review for me the way in which we divided up Canada for study?"

"Well, we had the history of Canada, the geography, and then we had one committee which looked at the effect of the history and geography on the products and industries."

"Good. I'm listing these here on the board. What else did we have?"

"We had one committee that studied people and customs, and one that studied relations with the United States."

"Is there anything else? I think that's about it. Notice that the same topics apply to both countries. If we find as we get into our study of Mexico that we need other categories, we can add them. Now . . . we have five committees here. How shall we divide up? Do you think it would be a good idea to have the same committees, or would you rather change to another area?"

"I think it would be good to stay with the same committee. Then we could learn more about the differences between the two countries."

"Well, I'd rather change. I'm not as interested in the effect of history and geography on products and industries as I am in the relations between Mexico and the United States."

Calls of "I'd like to switch," and "I want the same topic," were heard from various members of the class.

"It's pretty clear that some people want to change, while others want to stay with their former topic," commented Mr. Mitchell. "How about trying this solution? I'll ask for volunteers under each topic, and you can choose whatever you like. If there are too many for one or another of the committees, then we'll have to ask some people to make another choice. I would like to suggest, however, that we have at least one or two on each committee who had the same topic for Canada, because I think that would be helpful for comparisons, and also in getting off to a fast start. Okay—let's see how it goes. . . ."

ANALYSIS

1. How would you describe the verbal behavior of Mr. Mitchell and his class using VICS?

    a. Are the teaching questions broad or narrow?

    b. Are the pupil responses predictable or unpredictable?

    c. Does the teacher accept or reject pupil ideas?

    d. Find an example of teacher acceptance of pupil feeling.

2. To what extent are pupils involved in decision making in this situation?

    a. Who selected the topic and the subject matter to be emphasized?

    b. Who decided upon procedure for the study?

    c. What choices do pupils have?

3. Do you think that the class will look forward to this study, and if so, why?

SKILL SESSION Try to arouse the interest of a class in the study of a foreign country (select any country) by limiting your verbal behavior completely to the asking of questions. Accept and summarize all pupil responses in a role-playing session.

Try phrasing questions which encourage pupils to express their own opinions about the forthcoming unit.

Situation 7A

Mr. Jackson was reading off committee assignments to his seventh grade class. "And Jerry will work with Marjorie's group this time."

"Oh nuts," "Ugh," and "What luck!" were some of the remarks which came from the class.

"What's this? I don't think you people are being very polite," said Mr. Jackson. "You know that in this class we all work together and we all get along together."

"Oh yeah!" retorted Bill. "We don't all get along so well. Jerry is terrible to work with—and I'm saying that right to his face. He butts in all the time and he wants to do all the talking. He always has to be right."

"I agree with Bill," Mary joined in. "Jerry just doesn't know how to get along with anybody. He's always picking on somebody, and if he doesn't get his own way then he spoils it for everybody else. No wonder nobody wants to be on a committee with him."

"Now, now," said Mr. Jackson. "Sometimes we have to work with people who aren't our best friends, you know. I really am surprised to hear some of you talking the way you do. We all know that Jerry has many fine ideas. No one is perfect. Now let's divide up into our groups, and I don't want to hear any more complaints from anybody. We're all good sports here. Now let's get right to work."

ANALYSIS When the children in Mr. Jackson's class indicate that they do not want to work on a committee with Jerry, Mr. Jackson attempts to motivate the class to work with him by expressing disappointment in them for not meeting his standards for working with other children. He tells them to get to work and to work well together, and at the same time he lets them know that he doesn't want to hear about their not working well together.

Mr. Jackson doesn't utilize the children's initiated expressions of their feelings and ideas, other than to reprimand them, give his opinion of how they should behave, and give direction about how they ought to proceed. When children find that their expressed ideas and feelings are rejected by teachers, it is probable that they will not continue to openly share these opinions and feelings.

A skill session relevant to this situation will be found after situation 7C.

Situation 7B

Mr. Barrett read off the committee assignments to his seventh grade class. "This time Jack will work with Jean's group."

From several spots around the room were heard, "Aw heck," "Ugh," and "Poor us!"

"I hear some sounds of complaint," said Mr. Barrett. "What's the problem? Come on—don't be afraid to speak up. We'll see what we can do about things."

"Nobody wants to work with Jack, Mr. Barrett. He's such a pest, and he tries to run everything and he always wants his own way."

"Yeah—he's so hard to get along with. If you don't agree with him he has a fit. He spoils everything he's in."

"Jack—do you have anything to say for yourself?" asked Mr. Barrett.

"Aw, they're always complaining. Anyway, I don't care if no one wants to work with me. I'll work by myself, and I'll bet I do a better job than any of the committees anyway," responded Jack.

"That's not a very healthy attitude, Jack. This is committee work, and you have to join with one of the committees," Mr. Barrett said. "You know, I understand why the other boys and girls feel the way they do about you. You do think your ideas are the best, but you need to learn that other people have ideas too, and that if you're going to get along in this world you've got to share with others. Now you join the committee I assigned you to, and I don't want any trouble from you. If you have any trouble there, Jean, you just let me know. We're all going to be watching you, Jack, so you'd better get along."

ANALYSIS When the children in Mr. Barrett's class indicate that they do not want to work on a committee with Jack, one of their class members, Mr. Barrett attempts to motivate Jack to work in ways that are acceptable to the other class members by telling him that he must learn to get along with other people, and that there is to be no further trouble.

Mr. Barrett accepts the ideas and feelings of the class members who are complaining about Jack and uses these to reprimand Jack. He rejects Jack's reply after asking him if he has any defense. Jack may become less offensive to his classmates, but it is doubtful that his teacher has really helped him to become a positive, contributing, and accepted member of the group.

A skill session relevant to this situation is presented after situation 7C.

Situation 7C

Mr. Leavitt was finishing up the committee assignments in his seventh grade class. "Now let's see—Joe will be in George's group."

"Do we have to have him again?" and "Aw gee," came from the classroom.

"Well, I gather that some people have objections to working with you, Joe," said Mr. Leavitt.

"I don't care. I don't want to work with any of them anyway. I'd rather work by myself," responded Joe.

"Let's see if we can't talk a bit about this. I'd like to hear what some of the reasons are for not wanting to work with Joe," Mr. Leavitt requested.

"Well, he's always butting in when anyone else talks. And he thinks he's the only one who has any good ideas."

"Yeah, and if you don't agree with him he tells you you're dumb and you don't know anything."

"If he can't have his own way, he spoils things for everyone. No wonder we don't want to work with him."

"I guess you're saying," said Mr. Leavitt, "that working with people in groups can cause difficulty. People don't always agree with one another, and some committee members want their own way. And people sometimes think that their ideas are better than other people's ideas. In order for a group to work together, though, people have to listen to each other and sometimes change their own ideas or even give up their own ideas."

"Right! And Joe never gives up his own ideas."

Mr. Leavitt continued. "Why is it that people usually think the ideas they have are good ones? And have you noticed that some people give in more easily than others?"

"Yeah—my brother never gives in. What a pest!"

"Well I think that people think their own ideas are good just because they're theirs. Like you usually think your country is best, or your town."

"Well, I stick up for my ideas because I *really* think they're *good*," said Joe. "Otherwise I wouldn't suggest them. And you know, Mr. Leavitt, you've told me many times that I contribute some of the best suggestions in class. Some people really have more ideas or better ideas than other people, and if they're better than they should stick up for them."

"I guess we've all noticed that some people put up more of a fight for what they want to say than others," said Mr. Leavitt. "And certainly we've all noticed that some people talk much more than other people do. We know that in a democracy everyone should be allowed to contribute the best that he can, while at the same time considering the rights of others. In our groups we want to practice democracy—give everyone a chance to contribute, and utilize as many ideas and skills as we can. Does anyone have any suggestions for ways for working out the kind of problem we have been talking about here in class?"

"Well, what's the use of giving Joe a chance, he doesn't even want to change."

"Maybe we could try some role playing—you know, like we did last week about the kids picking on the other kids who can't play baseball too good. I liked that."

"All right," said Mr. Leavitt. "Any suggestions for situations?"

"Well, we could have the kids who are really on the committee with Joe go up and start to work together. Joe could play the chairman, and somebody else could play Joe."

"What do you say, Joe?" asked Mr. Leavitt.

"Well, I'll do it, but I'd still rather work alone," replied Joe.

"I think it might be good to give this a try, and then we'll decide," said Mr. Leavitt. "Who would like to be . . . ?"

ANALYSIS   When the children in Mr. Leavitt's class indicate that they do not want to work on a committee with one of their class members. Mr. Leavitt tries to motivate the class to work together with Joe by accepting the ideas and feelings of the class and of Joe, and by clarifying and building upon these expressions. He attempts to help the class see the essence of the problem, and asks for and acts upon suggestions for solving the problem.

Why is it likely that this class will continue to openly express their ideas and feelings to their teacher?

SUMMARY ANALYSIS, SITUATIONS 7A, 7B, 7C

In all three of these situations the teacher attempts to motivate a resistant class to work with a fellow class member whom they see as difficult. In each instance the class members initiate statements indicating their feelings and ideas to the teacher. Mr. Jackson, the teacher in situation 7A, rejects these statements of the class, and directs them to work better together. In situation 7B, Mr. Barrett accepts the statements of the class, but not the statements of the rejected child, and directs him to work better with the class. In situation 7C, Mr. Leavitt listens to and accepts and clarifies the ideas and feelings of the class *and* the rejected child.

In each case the teacher apparently makes different assumptions about the nature of the problem. Mr. Jackson appears to feel that the problem is rooted in the behavior and attitudes of the class rather than in the child about whom they complain. Mr. Barrett seems to feel that the problem results from the behavior of the individual child. Mr. Leavitt seems to think that the problem arises as a result of the behavior and feelings of both the class and the individual child. Certainly each teacher takes quite different action to attain his goal—that of motivating the class to work well together in groups.

SKILL SESSION   If a pupil says, "I don't want to work with Bill. He always spoils everything," one way that the teacher might accept the child's statement would be to say, "I guess you don't like working with Bill."

Think of accepting statements for the following expressions of feeling:

1. I don't want to work with this group anymore.
2. The kids in this group never give me any jobs to do.
3. The kids in this group aren't fair to me.
4. Why do we have to be in groups? I like it better when you teach all of us.

Sometimes teachers may want to accept some parts of children's statements and reject other parts. They may want to accept ideas and reject behavior, accept feeling and reject behavior, accept behavior and reject ideas, and so forth. For instance, if a pupil says, "I'm mad at Johnny. That's why I wouldn't let him help me on the bulletin board," a teacher might accept the feeling and reject the behavior in that statement by replying, "I understand that you're angry with Johnny, but everyone on the committee has a right to participate in the committee project."

Accept the feeling but reject the behavior in the following statements:

1. I don't want to work with those kids.
2. I don't like assemblies—that's why I talk to Joan.
3. I don't want to do my math.
4. Why do we have to wear sweaters for recess—we're not babies!
5. Committees are no fun. Why don't we just work all together?

Situation 8A

Most of the children in Mrs. Linton's eighth grade class consistently used such terms as "ain't," "he don't," and "we seen 'em," and Mrs. Linton decided upon a concerted effort to change their speech habits.

"You know, boys and girls," she said to her class one morning, "most of you use very poor English, and I've decided that we're going to get busy and do something about it. You're never going to get anywhere in school or in life speaking the way you do. Now, here's what we're going to do so that you'll learn to speak properly. Every day we're going to take some part of speech and we're going to talk about it, and learn the rule if there is one, and then we're going to write it ten times. Let's start with 'ain't.' What should we say instead of 'he ain't' or 'it ain't'?"

"We should say, 'he isn't' or 'it isn't.' "

"Good. Now today we're going to write 'I am not, you are not, he is not, she is not, it is not, we are not' and 'they are not' ten times each. Take out your notebooks and start copying while I write on the board."

"Mrs. Linton, I ain't got no notebook," came from Ruth. "My little brother, he scribbled all over it."

"That's not a very good start, Ruth," replied Mrs. Linton. "I just said that we aren't going to say 'ain't' anymore. It's poor English, and people who speak properly just don't use that word. You can tell people who are well educated by their speech—and you people don't sound educated at all! Now, get some paper from the cupboard, and remember what we just finished talking about!"

ANALYSIS

1. Identify Mrs. Linton's accepting and rejecting statements.
2. Are Mrs. Linton's rejecting statements mainly involved with ideas, behavior or feeling?
3. What seem to be some of Mrs. Linton's assumptions about how pupils are motivated?
4. What effects do you think Mrs. Linton's plan will have upon the youngsters and their speech, and why?
5. How else might Mrs. Linton attempt to motivate her pupils to change their speech habits?

SKILL SESSION   Learning theorists speak of the need for corrective feedback in learning. A teacher gives corrective feedback if a pupil gives the wrong answer and the teacher then gives him the right answer. For example, if a teacher asks, "What is four times three?" and a pupil responds by saying, "Four times three is seven," and the teacher then says, "Four *plus* three is seven, four *times* three is twelve," the teacher has given corrective feedback. Notice that the teacher in this example gives *only* corrective feedback; he includes no rejection. Teachers often tend to include rejecting statements along with their corrective feedback, especially when behavior is involved. When children are criticized they may be less motivated to incorporate into their future performance the corrective feedback which the teacher is attempting to provide.

                    Give corrective feedback which contains no rejection to the following pupil statements:

1. The capital of Pennsylvania is Philadelphia.
2. Blanket is spelled blanquet.
3. I ain't got no pencil.
4. Since Angle A equals 60°, the opposite angle equals 90°.

Situation 8B

Mrs. Benoit was concerned about the speech of her eighth grade class. She knew what a handicap their speech would be when it came to getting jobs or going on in school, and she decided to have a discussion with the class about the matter of English usage.

"You know, boys and girls, I thought it might be interesting if we spent some time studying about language—about how people talk to each other, how language may have started long ago when men were beginning to be what we think of as human; and we might even look a bit at some other languages to see how they are different from ours. For example, did you know that some languages have no plural nouns? That is, they don't have any way of distinguishing between one table and more than one. They can't say tables—only table. There are three table! It seems odd, doesn't it? But we have some nouns like that too. Can anyone think of a word that's the same whether we're talking about one or more than one?"

The class was silent, so Mrs. Benoit continued, "I'll give you a clue—where does wool come from?"

"Oh—sheep! Yeah. There are three sheep!"

"Yes. We don't say sheeps when we mean more than one, we use the word sheep for singular or plural—one or more than one. There are really lots of interesting things about language, and I'd like to get started with our study tomorrow. In the meantime, try thinking about how men might have first communicated with each other—before they had words.

"And," Mrs. Benoit went on, "along with our study of language and communication, I thought we might take a look at our own personal speech. Some of us have some speech habits that might be handicaps to us later on. What do I mean by that?"

"You might not get a good job if you don't talk right."

"And if you wanted to go to college or be a nurse or a teacher or sumpin' like that, you couldn't if you don't talk good."

"What do you mean by 'talk right' and 'talk good'?" asked Mrs. Benoit.

"They mean it ain't—I mean isn't—right if you say certain things. Like it ain't—I mean isn't—right to say 'ain't.' You should say 'is not.' "

"Will I understand you if you say, 'I ain't coming'?" asked Mrs. Benoit.

"Sure," "Natch," and "Of course," came from the class.

"Well then, why isn't it 'good' or 'right'?"

"It's not good because it don't sound too good. That's what our teacher said last year. It don't sound right and you should talk good English. 'Ain't' isn't good English."

"But why isn't it good English?" pursued Mrs. Benoit.

The class did not respond, so Mrs. Benoit continued. "Would you say that understanding what the other person means is the most important thing when we speak to each other?"

"Sure."

"Then what's wrong with saying 'ain't'?"

"Because teachers and other people said so."

"We seem to be saying that even though understanding each other is the most important thing when we speak to each other or communicate with each other, some people, like teachers, think that certain words are better or more correct or more appropriate than other words. And you are right about that. There aren't any absolute rules about what is right and what is wrong. That is, there is no book or person to tell us absolutely and forever that certain things are right and others wrong. Our language is constantly changing, and that's one of the things we'll want to look at in our study. Words that sound right to us may have sounded all wrong to people fifty years ago. But it is certainly true that some speech is more acceptable in some situations than others—even though the person you're speaking to may be able to understand you perfectly. You said that you might not be able to get a job, or might not be able to become a teacher or a nurse. And that's true. Because some language is more acceptable according to certain people's standards. For instance, suppose you went to apply for a job—maybe as a telephone repair man —and you said to the man, 'Well, I ain't had no trainin' in dis stuff, but I ain't afraid to try.' Who can say that in a way that would be more acceptable and might give you a better chance to get the job?"

"I haven't had no trainin' with these things, but I'd sure try," said one child.

"Naw—he should say, 'I haven't any trainin' with these things, but I'll try my best,' " said another.

"All right. What would you think of a project for this class that would help us to speak in ways that might make our lives better?" asked Mrs. Benoit. "That is, in ways that would help us get better jobs, and so forth."

"I'd like it," "I'm for that," "Okay," and "Yeah," came from several class members.

"Good," said Mrs. Benoit. "Now, I've been doing some reading about this. I can tell you that some people who spend their lives studying language—the experts—think that the best way to change speech is to practice out loud. They also say that one way that a class might work on change is to pick out one or two things and work on only these. That is, we could decide on one or two words and then we'd all try to change, and we could correct one another if we forget. What shall we pick as a start?"

"How about 'ain't,' since we keep sayin' that?"

"Fine. That's a good word to begin with. We're going to try to say, 'I am not, you are not' or 'you aren't, he isn't, we aren't,' and 'they aren't.' I'll put these over here on the board, and while I'm doing that, Lois, will you give me a sentence—anything—that uses one of these verbs?"

ANALYSIS

1. Identify Mrs. Benoit's accepting and rejecting statements.

2. Are Mrs. Benoit's accepting statements mainly involved with ideas, behavior or feeling?

3. What seem to be some of Mrs. Benoit's assumptions about how pupils are motivated?

4. What effects do you think Mrs. Benoit's plan will have upon the youngsters and their speech, and why?

Compare the verbal interaction in situations 8A and 8B. Compare the probable assumptions of these two teachers about how children are motivated.

SKILL SESSION   Teachers often accept pupil statements with such short responses as, "Good report," or "Nice work," or "Right." Sometimes giving reasons for this praise would increase teaching effectiveness. For example, "Good report," does not explain why the report is good. Presumably acceptance is motivational, so if the teacher includes reasons for the acceptance, the feedback to pupils will be more helpful and thus will have increased motivational effect on learning.

Expand or build on the following accepting statements by including reasons for the acceptance. For example, "Good report," might become "Your report was good because you talked to us instead of reading to us, and because your examples were so clearly related to our class work."

1. That's a good bulletin board.

2. Nice painting.

3. Good penmanship.

4. That's a clever story.

Situation 9

Mr. Lambert's ninth grade group was scheduled to begin a unit on the American political system, and he had timed this so that it would coincide with the local mayoralty election. He knew that his class probably wouldn't have too much information about the politics of their local community, but he hoped to use what information they had to spark an interest in the affairs of the wider community.

"I know that some of you have been looking at the local paper which we have here in our room," Mr. Lambert began, "and I wonder if anyone will tell us what event is going to take place in our town next week that the paper is devoting a lot of space to?"

"The Industrial League Series."

"That's true. I should have said, however, that I was thinking of the news on the front pages rather than the sports pages."

"Oh—there's gonna be an election."

"Okay. The voters are going to elect some city officials. What offices will be filled? That is, who will be elected?"

"How do we know—they ain't had the election yet!"

"I think you know what I meant, John," said Mr. Lambert. "I'm talking about the office, not which person or candidate will win the office. You seem to know something about this, John. What *is* the major office that will be filled?"

"They're gonna vote for mayor."

"And do you know the names of the candidates?"

"Yeah—Burrows and Fisher."

"I think you'll be a good resource person during this study, John. Now, all of you are familiar with voting. Your parents may have been talking about whom they're going to vote for."

"My old man said he ain't gonna vote. He said it don't matter who wins—they're all crooks."

"Well, my mother's gonna vote for Burrows 'cause my uncle works at City Hall."

"My father, he don't vote. Sometimes he votes for president, but he don't vote for mayor."

"You know, Bob, your father is like many other people. Many more people vote in the presidential elections than in the mayoralty elections. I'm going to put those two words, 'presidential' and 'mayoralty,' up on the board. Remember when we talked about local, state, and national government? Which of these elections would be local and which national? . . . Right," said Mr. Lambert, as the class responded.

"Now," Mr. Lambert continued, "we have already seen from the comments of the class that people have many reasons for voting and for not voting, as well. Did you know that in some countries people are fined if they don't vote? What do you think of that?"

"Good idea."

"Terrible."

"If I didn't want to vote, nobody could make me."

"Those of you who said good—why do you think that?" asked Mr. Lambert.

"Because, everybody should vote."

"It's their country and they should be interested."

"If they don't vote, they deserve what they get," came the responses.

"What about the people who said they thought fines weren't a good idea? How about you, Jenny?"

Well, I don't think it's a good idea, because if you're not interested, probably you wouldn't know anything about it, and you wouldn't vote for a good person."

"Both sides gave good reasons for their arguments," said Mr. Lambert. "In a few years you people will be able to vote, and you'll have to decide for yourselves whether or not to cast your ballots, and whether to vote for one candidate or another. Now—let's take some time here and now to have a mock election for mayor. We'll select a person from our own group whom we think would make a good mayor, a good leader. What do you think our first step should be?"

ANALYSIS   Analyze this case by:

1. Describing the teacher and pupil talk using the VICS.

2. Discussing the possible effects of the teacher's attempts to motivate the pupils to study the American political system.

3. Discussing the teacher's underlying assumptions about motivation.

SKILL SESSION   In order to consciously select the verbal behavior which you wish to use in your teaching, you must practice using a variety of teacher statements. Each teacher statement in this situation may be modified so that it will fall into a different VICS category. For instance, "And do you know the names of the candidates?" is a narrow question which Mr. Lambert asks after a pupil says, "They're gonna vote for mayor." He might have responded to that pupil statement by giving information, "The office of mayor is the highest elective office in our city," or by giving direction, "Would you please write the word 'mayor' at the top of the center blackboard?" or by asking a broad question, "Why do you think people have thought up the system of voting for leaders?" or by accepting the idea, "Yes. The voters of the city will go to the polls to elect a mayor," or by rejecting the behavior, "We don't say 'gonna,' we say 'going to,' " and so forth.

Practice various teacher verbal behaviors by reading each teacher statement in this situation and modifying it so that it will fall into several different VICS categories.

CHAPTER 4
Planning

Teaching is defined in this book as an interactive process, primarily involving classroom talk, which takes place between teacher and pupils and occurs during identifiable activities. The situations in this chapter, therefore, will consider planning as it occurs *between* teachers and pupils.

There are many ways to plan with pupils, from sharing teacher-made plans arrived at outside the classroom, to consulting with pupils about their thoughts and opinions before engaging in planning outside the classroom, to cooperative planning with pupils, to allowing pupils to plan completely independently. Some teachers almost never engage in planning as a teaching activity; that is, they do not even share with pupils the plans they have made independently, other than to say such things as, "Take your math books out next, and turn to page 37."

Teachers who involve children in planning have different goals from teachers who do not engage pupils in the planning process, whether or not their goals are consciously expressed. If a teacher truly believes that the process of planning is itself an important learning experience for children, then he will include his pupils in that process. If, on the other hand, a teacher believes that planning is not an important experience for children, or if he believes that since pupils are not as capable of planning for their classroom experiences as trained adults, they need not be involved, then he will plan for teaching without engaging pupils.

Perhaps if youngsters are actively participating in the planning process, they will not only take a more active interest in the curriculum, and acquire the skill of planning for learning, but they may also come to know that their own actions can make a difference in their lives—an important social and political learning. If one believes that a good citizen is one who actively participates in the affairs of the community, then it would seem that one would want pupils to engage actively in the planning of their classroom destinies

—so they will learn that the actions of individuals working together can make a difference. If all decisions are made *for* pupils, then they may be learning to be passive citizens. When the curriculum is so routine that it involves little more than the reading of textbooks and workbooks, and the exchange of cognitive-memory questions and answers, then there is little for either teachers or pupils to plan around.

The situations in this section, and their accompanying analyses and skill sessions, will allow you to look at several kinds of teacher-pupil planning, and will also permit you to extend your own capabilities in this teaching activity.

Situation 1

The kindergarten class had been taking a number of walks through their neighborhood, looking at the houses in which each class member lived, and noticing the stores and businesses which were nearby. Miss Blake, their teacher, thought it would be a good idea to set up a model of the neighborhood in the kindergarten block corner, and she discussed this with the class as they planned their morning activity period.

"We've been taking some walks around our neighborhood," she began, "and we've now seen everybody's house, and a lot of other things as well. I think it would be a good idea to try to make a little model of our neighborhood over in the block corner. We could have streets and stores and so forth just the way we saw them in our walks —using blocks and other things for buildings. Now . . . how do you think we could start?"

"Me and Bobby could do it. We're good builders and we made a good train station the other time."

"You are indeed good builders," said Miss Blake, "and you'll be able to do a lot on this project. But we want to do this together— everyone will have a chance to help."

"Well, we could have streets with cars and I can bring in my cars."

"I can make a picture of my house."

"My mother took us for a walk yesterday, and I showed her where Betty and Jackie live."

"Suppose I asked you people to take some visitor to our class on a walk around our neighborhood and show him everyone's house. Could you do it without any help?" asked Miss Blake.

"No," "I couldn't remember," "I could do it," "Sure," "It's too hard," came some responses from the children.

"Well, I think that some of us might remember quite a few houses, and could show them, but it would probably be hard to remember everything without some help. Can you think of something that might help?"

"We could ask everybody where they live."

"We might ask everybody," said Miss Blake, "and each person could tell his address. But then you still might have trouble remembering."

"We could take one kid from every street and then we'd know."

"That would be a way to solve it. And I can think of another way," added Miss Blake. "Have any of you ever heard of a map?"

"Sure, my father uses it in the car," "My sister has one in her book," "We have one in the den," the children responded.

"What is a map?" asked Miss Blake.

"It's like a picture—it tells you where to go," "You look at it and you know how to drive," "It tells about another country," came from the children.

"So a map is like a picture or chart that shows where certain things are. Sometimes we use maps when we go on car trips so we'll know which road to take. And sometimes we look at maps to find out about other cities or countries. Well, *we* can make a map of our neighborhood, and then we can look at it and tell where things are. We could tell where each of you live. It would be like a picture of our neighborhood. What else might be on our map?"

"The stores," "The laundry," "The streets."

"Good. Our houses and the businesses around us, and the streets. Now if we were really going to use our map to take a visitor around, we'd need a small map that we could carry. But we don't plan to do that, so we can make a great big map. We can use the mural paper that we have in the cupboard. I'll help you with the street names, and then we can use Mary's idea and each make a picture of our own house and put it in the proper place on the map. Then our map will help us with the model that we make in the block corner, because we can look at the map and then we'll know how to set up the model. I'm not sure that we'll have enough blocks, though. Do any of you have any ideas of other things we could use?"

"For buildings we can use boxes," "I can bring in cars," "I have a doll house we can use," "Me, too," responded the children.

"I heard some good ideas there," said Miss Blake. "Boxes can make good houses, especially shoe boxes, so perhaps some of you can bring some in. Or if you have other small boxes, or cars, or play people or houses, or anything you think might fit in well, bring it along. Now, remember, we're going to make a model in the block corner *and* a paper map. Today, I think we might draw pictures of our houses for the map. What else might we draw to paste onto our map?"

"The laundry," "The A & P," "The candy store," "The gas station," "The bakery."

"Good. And I can think of something else. A building where we spend a lot of our time about five days a week."

"THE SCHOOL!" came a loud chorus.

"Yes. Now, I'll get out the roll of mural paper, but I'll need some help in measuring off what we need and so forth, so I'd like Jean and Laura and Bobby and David L. to help with that while the rest of you start on your drawings. Will this week's chairmen please get the crayons and paper for your tables?"

ANALYSIS   This teacher begins by giving information and opinion and then asking a broad question. Then her verbal behavior often follows a pattern of accepting children's ideas, giving opinion and then asking a question. Her questions generally become more narrow as the lesson proceeds.

The children's talk includes both predictable and unpredictable responses. In response to Miss Blake's first question, "How do you think we could start?" all of the responses are unpredictable. Some are not directly relevant, such as, "I can make a picture of my house." A broad question usually precludes predictable responses. Even though we might say that "Me and Bobby could do it," and "Well, we could have streets with cars and I can bring in my cars," are not unexpected replies, they are classified as unpredictable responses because the range of student suggestions in response to the initial question is so broad that its limits cannot easily be identified.

"What is a map?" elicits more predictable responses, such as, "It's like a picture—it tells you where to go." The question is narrow because the range of responses has limits which can be identified fairly well. It would be possible to have an unpredictable response for a narrow question such as "What is a map?" only if the response does not directly answer the question, as for example, "I had a map once." It is probably not possible to get directly relevant unpredictable responses to truly narrow questions.

This teacher apparently believes that children should be included in some aspects of planning. She has decided on the activity and she shares the plans with the children, involving them in a discussion of how they might go about making a neighborhood model and map. Miss Blake has involved these young children in limited yet active planning in a way that should allow them to work with interest on this project.

SKILL SESSION Accept the following pupil responses to teacher questions, even though they are not directly relevant to the question asked.

Teacher	What are some of the things we might do at our party?
Pupils	I had a birthday party last year.
	Who is coming to our party?
	I can ask my mother to make a cake.
	I like to have parties.
Teacher	Do you think you can play musical chairs without making a lot of noise?
Pupils	I don't like that game.
	We used to play that last year.
	Can I be the one to take the needle off the record?
Teacher	What might we show in our mural?
Pupils	I don't know what a mural is.
	I'm a good painter.
	Can I help put the paper on the wall?
	The sixth grade has a mural out in the hall.

Situation 2A

Mrs. Fowler's second grade class was going to the dairy farm in two days and she thought they needed to begin planning rather specifically about what information they might get at the farm. She also wanted the class to review their trip behavior standards.

"Everyone has already brought in permission slips for our trip to the dairy farm," Mrs. Fowler began, "and we've made arrangements with the bus company and the farmer, and three mothers have volunteered to go along with us. So we're just about set. Does anyone remember what else we did when we went on the trip to the post office? Val?"

"We made a list of rules for behaving, and we thought up questions we wanted to ask the postmen."

"Exactly. Now—let's review the rules we made that time for behavior on the bus. John?"

"We said the best way to keep together is to have a partner. Do we have to have the same partner?"

"Well, I did think that having a partner worked well, and I'm going to ask everyone to stay with his partner again, as you did last time. Let's see. Later today I'll ask you to write down three choices for a partner, and tonight I'll take the papers home with me, and I'll try to give everyone one of his choices for a partner. But you'll have to remember that it isn't possible to work it out exactly, so you may be disappointed. I believe that you're all polite enough to take any disappointment like good sports, however. Okay? Now are there any other rules we can remember besides staying with your partner on the bus and at the farm? Lois?"

"We were supposed to talk quiet on the bus, but I think some people were too noisy."

"One of our rules was to speak quietly on the bus," Mrs. Fowler agreed. "One thing that might help is to remember to talk just to your partner or to people who are very close to you. If you try to say something to someone who's far away, what happens?"

"You have to yell, and then nobody can hear and everybody has to yell."

"But if everyone cooperates, then everyone can hear and can talk easily to his neighbors. Any other rules?" asked Mrs. Fowler.

"Don't stand up and don't push."

"All right. Let's remember to stay in our seats, and to get on and off the bus carefully. I'm sure that everyone knows the reason for this. Any others? I think that's about what we had last time. I have the chart we made then, and I'll take it out when we finish the rest of our planning."

"Now," she continued, "let's think about some of the things we'd like to find out while we're at the farm. Who'd like to make some suggestions? Jimmy?"

"I'd like to try to milk a cow." "Me, too." "I would too."

"We can certainly ask the farmer if he'll let us try. But perhaps it won't be milking time when we're there. Does anyone know about that?"

"Well, I think they only milk the cows at night. And I'm going to be a farmer, so I could ask the farmer how you get to be one."

"We could ask the farmer to tell us how you learn to be a farmer," agreed Mrs. Fowler, "and I think we'd better check on just when cows are milked—and how often. Any other things?"

"I'd like to know the names of the cows, and I want to see the baby cows. I saw a baby cow at the fair last year."

"Suppose I begin making this list on the board," suggested Mrs. Fowler. "1. Can we try milking a cow? 2. How do you learn to be a farmer? 3. When are cows milked and how many times a day are they milked? 4. Do cows have names? 5. Are there any calves on the farm? And I'd like to have him tell us about what the milk is put into after it comes from the cow, and where it goes between the time it leaves the farm and the time we buy it in the store or the milkman brings it to our house. Any others you want?"

"Let's ask him what he grows on the farm."

"All right—that's number eight. Anything else? Nothing we can think of right now? Well, we have another day before we go in case we think of anything else. We'll talk about this again tomorrow. Now I'm going to get our old bus behavior chart out and we'll read it over, and we'll read over these questions. While we're doing that who would like to copy down some of the questions so that we have them before the board is erased? Let's have Teddy do one and two, Janet do three and four and Henry take five and. . . ."

ANALYSIS In this situation the pattern of questions and responses is rather different when the class discusses rules for behavior from when they discuss what they would like to find out at the farm. Describe and discuss these differences by referring to the categories in the VICS.

Further analysis, and a relevant skill session will be found after situation 2B.

Situation 2B

Mrs. Granger's second grade class would be going to the dairy farm the next morning, and she wanted to be sure that they knew in advance what to look for and how to behave.

"I have everybody's permission slip now," said Mrs. Granger, "and so we're all ready to take our trip to the dairy farm. You all have been on bus trips before, and you know how to behave. But just for review I've put a few rules here on this chart. Let's read it together."

ON THE BUS

1. Sit quietly.
2. Talk quietly.
3. Remain seated during the ride.
4. Get on and off the bus carefully.

"Before we leave, each of you will have a partner, and I'd like you to sit on the bus with your partner and stay with him as we go around the farm. And we'll have to be very careful about our line. We will have several mothers with us, and of course I know that you will listen to them as carefully as you always do to me. I'm sure we won't have any problems about behavior, and I'm counting on you to be good boys and girls so I can be proud of you.

"Now, let's think about some of the things we want to look for and think about when we get there. The farmer will be there and we'll be able to ask questions. It would be a good idea to get some questions out now, so that we'll remember what we want to find out. I'll write "Things to Find Out at the Farm" here on the board, and we can put our questions underneath. Who wants to start? Joey?"

"I want to find out how to be a farmer."

"Carol?"

"Let's ask him if we can milk a cow."

"Well, these aren't the kinds of questions I had in mind. I think it would be nice if we asked him how often his cows are milked, and where they send the milk after it leaves the farm, and what cows eat —questions like that. Let me put those down. And, oh yes, let's have him tell us what kind of containers the milk is sent out in. And another good question would be whether cows eat different food in summer from what they eat in winter. Now, this is a good beginning. Does anyone have anything else?"

"Let's ask him what he grows there."

"Well, this is a dairy farm, so let's just stick to questions about milk and cows."

"Will there be any baby cows there?"

"I don't know," replied Mrs. Granger. "We can see when we're there. Any more questions? I think we have a good number here. All right, I'll copy these down later, and take them with us. Well, I think that now we're really ready for our trip tomorrow."

ANALYSIS   The teachers in situations 2A and 2B approach the same kind of activity, a trip to a dairy farm, quite differently. Mrs. Fowler, the teacher in situation 2A asks a series of narrow questions to review the rules for behavior and the reasons for these rules, while Mrs. Granger, the teacher in situation 2B, has the children read the rules from a chart, following this with some direction and opinion. Mrs. Granger states her opinion that she's sure there won't be any problems about behavior because she is counting on them to be good so that she can be proud of them. Mrs. Fowler helps the class define some rules using public criteria to determine proper behavior for their bus ride.

Notice the different ways in which these teachers handle pupil comments dealing with a desire to milk a cow or be a farmer. Mrs. Fowler accepts these ideas, while Mrs. Granger rejects them by saying, "These aren't the kinds of questions I had in mind."

Mrs. Fowler asks some children to copy down the questions so that "We'll have them before the board is erased," while Mrs. Granger says, "I'll copy these down and take them with us."

In what ways do Mrs. Fowler's assumptions about the role of pupils in planning appear to differ from those of Mrs. Granger? What will be the possible consequences of these two planning sessions in terms of the trip, and in terms of the children's participation in any future planning with the teacher?

SKILL SESSION   Role play a situation in which a teacher and a class plan a trip to the local firehouse. The teacher will accept and build upon all pupil contributions in this pupil-teacher planning session.

Situation 3

The children in Mrs. O'Brian's third grade class had written many of the books which they used for reading. They dictated their stories to Mrs. O'Brian, who wrote them down in book form, and the children did the illustrations. The program had been very successful.

"You know, boys and girls," said Mrs. O'Brien one day, "I believe that you ought to show your books to some of the other classes. They're so interesting that I think others would like to see them. What do you think?"

"Yeah—let's show 'em to the other kids."

"We could tell 'em to come to our room like those other times."

"Which classes shall we invite?" asked Mrs. O'Brian.

"We could invite 'em all."

"We could have the little kids."

"Invite Mr. Paul's class. My sister's got him."

"The other third grades."

"Perhaps before we decide which classes to invite, we ought to decide what we're going to do after they arrive," suggested Mrs. O'Brian. "That might help us when we think about whom to invite."

"We could have the books around and everybody could look."

"The little kids can't read, so they can't come."

"We could read to them."

"Yeah—let's read some of the books."

"I hear two ideas coming out," Mrs. O'Brian said. "It's been suggested that we have some of the books on display around the room so that the visitors can look at them, and also that we might read some of the books aloud. Both good ideas, I think, and certainly we can do both. Now let's get back to the question of whom to invite."

"I like the little kids. Let's ask kindergarten kids."

"Could our mothers come?"

"We could ask the principal."

"I want Mr. Paul's class, so my sister can come."

"Yeah—how about Mrs. Broudy's class? My brother's in there."

"How would we fit all of these people in here?" asked Mrs. O'Brian.

"That's right. They ain't gonna fit."

"They don't all have to come together, ya know."

"Perhaps we can have several different groups," agreed Mrs. O'Brian, "each at a different time. And we might invite all your brothers and sisters who are in our school, even if we don't invite their classes. I think their teachers would be willing to let them come. Maybe we could invite mothers and grandmothers and fathers or any other relatives who want to come, at the same time that we have brothers and sisters. How would that be?"

"Yeah, that's good."

"My mother can't come."

"Well, not everyone will have mothers or any other family member here. Some of you will and some won't. However, whoever comes will be the guests of everyone. Remember when we talked about being hosts and guests? Well, we're all hosts and everyone who comes will be guests of the whole class."

"Can we have the kindergarten kids that had us to the band concert?"

"Yeah, we oughta have them."

"I agree that it would be nice to invite that class. So far, then, we have two groups; relatives and the kindergarten. I think we'd better have only one more group," said Mrs. O'Brian.

"Then let's have Mrs. Ungar's third grade kids."

"Yeah, we know them kids best."

"Fine. Then that will be the three groups. Perhaps we had better plan to have the relatives last. Then we could have the kindergarten in the morning, because that group is only here in the morning, and we could have the other third grade in the afternoon of the same day. The next day we can have the families. Shall we have them in the morning or afternoon? We can invite younger brothers and sisters if there's no one to leave them with."

"My sister takes a nap in the afternoon so my mother can't come then."

"Mine too."

"My mother works, so she can't come anyway."

"Perhaps it will be a good idea to have the family group in the morning, since several people have younger brothers and sisters who might nap. Anyone think afternoon is better? No one? All right. Now, what will our next steps be?"

"What about the principal?"

"Oh yes. Better ask him along with the third grade class. Now, what next?" asked Mrs. O'Brian.

"We gotta write letters to tell them."

"And we gotta fix the room."

"And decide the books to read."

"We certainly do have to invite the people we want. How many have brothers or sisters in the school whom you'd like to invite? Then you people can be responsible for sending invitations to them," Mrs. O'Brian went on.

"But I have three sisters and brothers."

"That's right. Some have more than one. Well, we'll all help out with those invitations. And we need to invite family members from home. Even if we're not sure they can come, we'll invite all our families. And we have to invite the third grade and the kindergarten. We can decide together what the invitations should say. Can the invitations all say the same thing?" asked Mrs. O'Brian.

"Yeah, sure."

"Naw. The day is different."

"Perhaps we'd better make up four kinds of invitations. One for families at home, one for brothers and sisters here at school, one for the third grade and one for the kindergarten," suggested Mrs. O'Brian. "We only need to send one copy for the whole class to the kindergarten and third grade. So let's start by doing those. And after we decide what to say on the invitation for families, it would be best to have it dittoed. We'll do those tomorrow, so you can think about what you want to say in the meantime. And you can also begin to think about how we will decide which books to read. Will we pick different books for different groups? We'll need to talk about that. When families come we can have some time for people to show their own books to their families."

"Let's have food."

"Oh boy! Let's have cake and ice cream."

"I think we'd better just concentrate on showing our books. Well —when the families come we might serve something nice to drink— some lemonade, maybe. Now," Mrs. O'Brian continued, "when do you think we can be ready for our book show . . . ?"

ANALYSIS   Notice that this teacher deliberately encourages pupil-initiated talk which includes unpredictable pupil responses as well as pupil-to-pupil responses. She directs the flow of discussion by building her questions and statements of information or opinion on student ideas, which she summarizes. In this way she incorporates pupil ideas into the planning session.

Sometimes one hears educators say that teachers should not repeat children's statements, giving as their reason that children will not listen to each other if the teacher repeats what they say. However, there is no evidence to back up this advice, and in fact, there is evidence which indicates that superior teachers do repeat and rephrase what children say, by reflecting their feelings, by summarizing their ideas and by restating their ideas in more cogent form.[1]

Notice that Mrs. O'Brian sometimes uses statements which evoke student talk even though they are not questions. For example, she says, "Perhaps before we decide which classes to invite, we ought to decide what we're going to do after they arrive. That might help us when we think about whom to invite." State-

---

1 Ned A. Flanders, *Teacher Influence, Pupil Attitudes, and Achievement,* U.S. Department of Health, Education and Welfare, Office of Education, Cooperative Research Monograph no. 12 (Washington, D.C.: U.S. Government Printing Office, 1965), p. 114.

ments of information or opinion can cause children to ask questions. For instance, a teacher might say, "I wonder about what this author says," or "I'm just not sure of that," or "I find that very interesting," and then pause for pupil responses.

SKILL SESSION   It is possible to have a group conversation in which few teacher questions are asked, but this is a difficult skill which takes practice to attain. Role play a conversation on any topic with another person in which neither of you asks any question. You might divide into groups of three, with one person as an observer, and the other two as the discussants, and after a few minutes change roles.

Situation 4

It was the fourth grade's turn to present an assembly program, and Mr. Graff decided that it would be a good idea to give a play. He had found a good one in the library about pioneer days, and since the class had been learning some square dances and folk songs, they could work the dances and songs into the play. The class knew that next month was their assembly turn, and Mr. Graff had asked them to think about things they might like to do, so that they could discuss the matter together.

"Remember yesterday I reminded you that next month we were responsible for an assembly program, and I asked you to think about what we might do. Any ideas?"

"I liked the stories with pictures that the fifth grade class did. Maybe we could do something like that."

"Let's get out as many ideas as possible before we discuss them," said Mr. Graff, "and then we'll see what might be best. Patsy?"

"Last year we did a movie—we made lots of pictures and pasted them together and then turned the rollers, and told the story. That was fun."

"Nancy?"

"How about a play? I have a good idea for one. We could. . . ."

"A play strikes me as being a very good idea, Nancy," said Mr. Graff. "We haven't done one yet this year, and we haven't seen too many, either. And there's always plenty for everyone to do in a play. How many would like to have a play? Good—then that's settled. Now, what kind of play do you think we should have? Nancy?"

"Well, I have an idea already. I thought about it yesterday, and me and some of the other kids started making up a play. It would be like a television show, and we'd act out stories about kids and animals —like Lassie."

"Well, I think it would be too difficult to have a play that had animals, Nancy, but I'm glad you were thinking about it," said Mr. Graff. "Perhaps we could have some kind of play about olden days."

"Yeah!" said Jack. "We could have it about kings and queens, with knights and stuff. And we could carry spears."

"That's a good idea, but I was thinking about the early days of *this* country," said Mr. Graff. "The pioneer days. You know we could use the square dances you've been learning, because those were the kinds of dances people used to do in those days. And we know some good folk songs that people used to sing then. What do you think? I think it would be fun, and the audience would enjoy it. How many like the idea of a play about pioneer days? I see lots of agreement. Now, I have a book of plays and one is about the pioneers. Let me read it to you, and see what you think."

ANALYSIS   Examine this teacher's questions and note particularly his responses to the student's ideas which his questions evoke. He has a frequent pattern of responding to pupil statements with some acceptance and some rejection. There would seem to be little difference between the plan Mr. Graff develops with the class and the one he might have developed by himself. Do you think there is a place for this kind of planning in teaching?

What assumptions does Mr. Graff seem to hold about the role of pupil participation in the planning process?

These children may feel that they are being consulted, and they may well enjoy the play—but what have they missed in this planning session?

SKILL SESSION

1. Role play with a group a session in which the teacher asks for suggestions and rejects none, but accepts and supports only those with which he agrees. The teacher should initially state that he has no personal preference for any plan (though he really does). Discuss the group's feelings at the end of the session. The group might be planning for a culmination to a certain unit, for a parent night enter-

tainment, for a theme for a concert of songs, for a next topic of study in science, or for anything they wish to choose.

2. Role play with a group a session in which the teacher tells the class that he is going to try to influence them toward a certain point of view or course of action in planning. The teacher will give his opinion and ask for other suggestions. He will reject no suggestions, but accept and support only those with which he agrees. Discuss the group's feelings at the end of the session.

Situation 5A

"Our next science unit deals with the history of the earth, and I want to spend some time this afternoon planning the unit with you," said Mr. Tyler to his fifth grade class. "What do you think will be involved in this topic, the earth's history? Will we be talking about how this planet began—will we be talking about the history of different countries? What will we be covering?"

"We'll be talking about how this planet began."

"Right. Since this is science rather than social studies we won't be dealing with the history of countries. We'll be looking back into the earth's beginnings and dealing with certain questions such as what the earth was like before any life existed on it, whether or not the seas and land masses were always in the same places, how we think life arose, and so forth. Do you think that in this unit we'll be talking about the other solar systems, or will we mention only our own?"

"Only our own."

"Yes. We might want to examine the relationship between our planet and the others in our solar system, but we won't be studying other possible solar systems. Now, there are a variety of reasons why it's important to study about the earth. Our planet is not a finished product; that is, it is still changing and will undoubtedly continue to change. The more we know about the past, the more we can know about the present and perhaps predict the future. What, then, is one important reason for studying about the earth's history?"

"Well, if you study about what happened a long time ago, you might know more about the earth today, and about what can happen in the future."

"Very good. Our science book has some excellent material, and some of us can be on a library committee to get other materials. We have about three weeks for this unit, and I'd like everyone to get busy as soon as possible. I think we might make some charts showing how the earth might have looked at different times, and perhaps we can have some rock displays. During this unit I've decided that we should have a brief quiz every Wednesday and Friday, so that we don't have to wait until the end of the unit to check on what we've learned. Today I want everyone to take out his science book and read the first ten pages beginning with page 118, and then we'll discuss what we've read. Does anyone have any additional suggestions? If you do, don't hesitate to bring them to me. Now, let's take out our books."

ANALYSIS This teacher's verbal behavior consists mainly of giving information and opinion. He exerts a great degree of control over his pupils' verbal behavior by asking extremely narrow questions about information he has already supplied. His questions are worded in such a manner that the response he receives is almost inevitable. He then accepts these pupil responses with the brief comments, "Right," "Yes," "Very good."

Why do you think it is that the pupils have no response to his question, "Does anyone have any additional suggestions?"

SKILL SESSION Take each of Mr. Tyler's questions and modify them so that pupils would *have* to give unpredictable responses.

Situation 5B

Mr. Bellows was speaking to his fifth grade class. "Our next science unit is entitled, 'The History of the Earth'—some of you have noticed it in our science books already, I'm sure. But if this is a science unit, why are we talking about history? What do you think that history has to do with science here?"

There was no response from the class, so Mr. Bellows continued. "What is history, anyway?"

"It's learning about olden days," "About the past," "It's studying about how things used to be," came some responses.

"Why do we study history?" asked Mr. Bellows.

"To learn about the past."

"Yes. And why do we want to learn about the past? What is the purpose?"

"Well, it's interesting to know what happened a long time ago," came from one student.

"And it can help you today. You might not make some mistakes or you might know how to do things better," said another.

"We seem to be saying," said Mr. Bellows, "that we study history in order to learn about the past, and we want to learn about the past because it can help us to know about the present, and perhaps even the future. We might be able to solve problems if we have a knowledge of history—but it's interesting to just learn about how things used to be. Those are all good points. Now, tell me a bit more about the word 'history' here in science period."

"You can have a history of anything. My sister has a history of fashions book, and it's all about clothes."

"Yeah—we have a book at home about the history of the movies."

"So history can be applied to many things besides countries," said Mr. Bellows. "I took a simple definition from Webster's dictionary, which I'll put up here on the board. History is 'that branch of knowledge that records and explains past events.' Notice the word 'explains' —that's an important word. History is a subject that tells about things that happened, and attempts to explain why they happened."

"You know, Mr. Bellows, this class has a history, too."

"Yes. If we wanted to, we could go back and reconstruct the things that have happened in our fifth grade, and we could write them down and try to interpret and explain them, and we'd have a history of Class 5, Room 16. And we would be historians. In fact, if some of you want to do that for a composition project we can talk about it. Now—what are some of the things we'll probably be studying about in our unit on the history of the earth?"

"How the earth began," "What made it," "How did it get here," "What was it like a billion years ago," came from the children.

"About all those things," agreed Mr. Bellows. "How the earth has differed over the ages, how it might have begun. Think about our definition of history."

"We'll be studying about the earth a long time ago and we'll try to explain it."

"Yes—and you know, history doesn't only deal with 'long ago.' What happened yesterday is history. Now," continued Mr. Bellows, "how might we begin our study?"

"We could read the part in our science books that tells about it. Then we can think up more questions and look in other books."

"That would be one way to begin," said Mr. Bellows. "Then we can use the material that we have on hand right now. Let's look ahead and see what else we can do to find out about the history of the earth."

"We can look in that film catalog you have, and maybe there are some good movies about the earth," said one youngster.

"I know there are," another joined in, "because I saw one on television. I'd remember the name if I saw it."

"I saw a good show on TV about the end of the earth," said someone else. "I could write a story about that."

"That's not history—what's *going* to happen!"

"Oh yeah—well, even Mr. Bellows said that we study history to know about the future. I saw a program about the sun and they said some day the sun would die, and then the earth would die—in a million years, or something like that."

"Certainly it might be interesting to see if we can use what we learn from our study of the past to look into the future. Scientists do that, you know," commented Mr. Bellows. "Perhaps we've talked enough for today. Tomorrow we'll plan in more detail. In the meantime who wants to be on the library committee? You'll have to get permission to come home a little late so that we can go to the library after school tomorrow. All right—you five people who have your hands raised, bring notes saying that you can go. And anyone who has books at home, or any good materials, bring them in. Now, we have about ten minutes left, so let's begin reading the material in our science texts."

ANALYSIS   Notice that Mr. Bellows accepts and builds on or expands pupil contributions without using statements which are thought of as praise—such as "Good," "Right," and so forth. Some authorities believe that teachers should use both praise and criticism sparingly; rather that teachers should accept pupils' contributions by building them into the discussion framework. So acceptance and praise are not synonymous, although praise would be categorized under the Verbal Interaction Category of acceptance.

This is not to say that teachers should ignore the desire of pupils to please the teacher. Encouragement from the teacher need not be in terms of right rather than wrong, or good rather than bad according to the teacher's opinions. Encouragement may be given in terms of the pupil's *efforts,* the pupil's *contributions.*

Discuss the consequences of the approach to planning a new unit used by this teacher and that used by the teacher in situation 5A in terms of effect on pupils' learning to plan for their own learning.

SKILL SESSION Role play the beginning planning of a unit on the study of weather, in which the teacher accepts and encourages pupil contributions without using words of praise.

Situation 6A

"We have a few plans to make this morning, boys and girls," Miss Baer announced to her sixth graders. "We ought to establish a deadline for our group reports in social studies. How many more days do we need?"

"Our group needs more time. About two days, at least."

"So does ours. We might even need three days."

"Let's see, today is Tuesday. Can we say that Friday afternoon will be devoted to our reports? Does anyone need less than two days to work? Then, let's say that today and tomorrow we'll spend from 1:30 to 2:30 on reports," Miss Baer said. "After that some of the groups may be ready for something else."

"Can we go over the math homework?" asked one youngster. "I couldn't do some of the examples. Even my father couldn't do them."

"I couldn't do them either," another youngster joined in.

"How many want to review the math problems?" asked Miss Baer. "Everybody! Well, we better see what happened. During math time today, then, we'll review our work of the past few days. Remember that we won't be having any writing or spelling time today because Mr. Foster's class has invited us to see a play. Otherwise the program will be the usual one. Any comments? All right, then, let's get started. . . ."

ANALYSIS Identify the pupil-initiated statements in this case. Did you know that teachers often reject pupil-initiated comments, and the result is that most youngsters learn not to initiate conversation with teachers? Perhaps teachers feel uncomfortable about having their plans take an unexpected turn, and so they unconsciously teach children that initiation comes from the teacher, not from pupils.

SKILL SESSION   Respond to the following pupil-initiated statements
with acceptance:

Teacher   Open your spelling books to page 40.
Pupil   You said we could work on our stories today.

Teacher   No one knows how the universe began.
Pupil   My father said that the big bang theory is pretty well proved
now.

Teacher   Jane, would you take this to the office?
Pupil   Why does Jane always get a turn?

Pupil   Why do you always wear that sweater?
Pupil   How old are you?
Pupil   Do you smoke?
Pupil   I liked science better last year.
Pupil   You don't make your "g's" the right way.

Situation 6B

"Time to decide on our plans for the day,
boys and girls," said Miss Phinney to her sixth grade class. "What
shall I put first?"

"Opening exercises."

"All right," said Miss Phinney as she wrote that on the board.
"And then?"

"Math."

"Remember, this is Tuesday."

"Oh yeah—music."

"Right. And what next?" asked Miss Phinney.

"Individualized reading."

"Good. Then what?"

"Recess, then math, and then lunch."

"And what about this afternoon?" continued Miss Phinney. "What
shall we plan for that part of the day?"

"Social studies."

"Yes. And what else?"

"How about finishing the things we started in art?"

"You know we don't have art today. Is this Wednesday? After
social studies we have . . . ?"

"Science."

"Yes. And what shall we do after that . . . ?"

ANALYSIS

1. Describe and discuss the pupil-teacher interaction in this situation by referring to the categories in the VICS.
2. Compare this teacher's underlying assumptions about pupil-teacher planning with those of the teacher in situation 5A.
3. Compare the probable consequences of both teachers' planning sessions on increasing their pupils' ability to plan efficiently.

SKILL SESSION   Role play the planning of a class trip to a printing plant. In the first session the teacher should accept and build on all contributions, listing them on the board. The teacher will avoid judging whether or not he thinks the contributions are good or bad, but will use such verbal behavior as, "That's one idea," "I'll put that suggestion next," "Your suggestion is related to Howard's, so it can go over here," and so forth. Actually complete the planning session, deciding whatever needs to be decided.

In the second session the teacher will have decided on a plan beforehand, and will give information and opinion and ask only narrow questions which relate to the fulfillment of his plan.

Compare the two planning sessions.

Situation 7A

The youngsters in Miss Baer's sixth grade who were planning to report on UNESCO as part of a study of the United Nations were meeting together.

"I got these pictures that I sent for from UNESCO and they show children from other countries going to school. I think they're great and we can probably use them in our report," Norma began as she showed the other children her pictures.

"I like them too," agreed Anita, "and I'm sure we can use them. But remember the other day we said it would be good if we could have a debate and each represent a different country? Well—what would we debate?"

"We could debate whether UNESCO is a good organization or not," suggested Dorothy.

"Don't be silly. We wouldn't be debating if our organization is good or not if we're the organization," said Jeff.

"Then what will we debate? I'd like to have a debate," said Anita.

"Well, so would I," added Dick.

"Me too. But I can't think of anything," said Norma.

"Let's ask Miss Baer to help us. Can you come over here, Miss Baer?" called Anita.

"How are you coming?" asked Miss Baer as she walked over to join the group. "This is the group on the history of international organizations, isn't it?"

"No. We're UNESCO."

"Oh yes. How could I have made that mistake! I should know that wherever Norma is there'll be something about education and schools. What good pictures these are! I haven't seen them before. Now—what's the problem?" asked Miss Baer.

"We'd like to have a debate, and maybe take the parts of different countries, but we can't think of anything to debate," said Jeff.

"Well, you have these fine pictures of schools and children around the world. Perhaps you could do something with them," suggested Miss Baer.

"But what could we do with them? We were thinking of a panel about UNESCO."

"Can you think of questions about education and schools that UNESCO might debate? Remember, anything to do with education is within the scope of UNESCO's work."

"You mean like what should schools be like?" asked Dorothy.

"And who should go to school?" added Norma.

"Well, everybody should go," said Jeff.

"We think that now in this country—at least that everyone should go to school until a certain age or until they finish high school. But that wasn't always true, and it isn't true in many other countries now," commented Miss Baer.

"How about debating what people ought to learn when they go to school?"

"That's another good question. Why don't you raise a few more questions and get all of them down on paper and see how you feel about what sides you'd like to represent? Remember that you don't have to agree personally with the ideas in order to defend them in a debate. And perhaps before or after your debate you could have some kind of background reporting on the development of education and schools from quite early times, and the place of an organization like UNESCO in the further development of education. Well, another group is paging me," said Miss Baer as she arose, "and I think you have enough to go on for awhile. Check with me later."

ANALYSIS   When a teacher uses group work in his teaching, the way in which he interacts with each group has significant effect upon the success of the work. Describe and discuss this teacher's interaction with the group in the situation, using the VICS.

SKILL SESSION   Divide into groups of six to eight, and have one person in each group role play the part of the teacher. Each group will discuss plans for presenting a report on the work of the three branches of the federal government, and the teacher will speak only in order to clarify and expand the ideas of the pupils.

Situation 7B

Miss Phinney had divided her sixth grade class into four groups to present reports on the United Nations and had assigned topics to each group, dividing the children alphabetically. During social studies time the group which was to include the work of UNESCO in their report was meeting around the library table.

"I can't think of any special way to present our report," began Marion. "Miss Phinney said we should think of interesting things to do."

"Why don't we have a panel like on TV? That's what one of the other classes is doing, because Anita Young told me about it," reported Jack. "They're going to discuss problems about education."

"Yeah, but that isn't about UNESCO," commented Dick.

"We're supposed to report on what UNESCO does, not on problems of education," agreed Barbara. "I looked up the UN in my encyclopedia last night and copied down what it said."

"We have these books that Miss Phinney gave us," said Dick. "We can get some good stuff from them. Maybe we could make a book out of our reports like last time. Anyway, here comes Miss Phinney, and she'll tell us what will be good."

"How are you coming along, boys and girls?" asked Miss Phinney as she pulled a chair up to their group. "This is the group that has UNESCO to report on, isn't it? Well, you have a lot of interesting material to work with. What kind of report have you decided to give?"

"We didn't decide yet, but I thought maybe we could have a debate," said Jack.

"And what would you debate? What question?" asked Miss Phinney.

"Well, maybe something about the importance of education, because UNESCO is interested in education."

"But you're really supposed to report on the work of UNESCO, aren't you? What the function of the organization is. So you had better give a straight report on that—not go off on another subject. Maybe you could have some charts, and perhaps you could put your material in a nice book for the bulletin board," suggested Miss Phinney. "And remember, when you read your reports to the class, use good clear voices so everyone can hear. Now are you all set? Good—you can start writing."

ANALYSIS

1. Describe and discuss the talk in this situation by referring to the categories in the VICS.
2. Compare the underlying assumptions of the teacher in situation 7A with those of the teacher in situation 7B about working with small groups.
3. Compare the consequences of these two teachers' methods of working with groups on the pupils' abilities to plan for independent group work.

SKILL SESSION   Divide into groups of six to eight and have one person in each group role play the part of the teacher. Each group will discuss plans for presenting a report on the work of the three branches of the federal government, and the teacher will give direction and opinion to the group as they make their plans.
              Compare the effects of the teacher's behavior on these groups with the skill session groups in situation 7A.

Situation 8

              Mr. Roberts' seventh grade science class was preparing to look at some cell slides under microscopes. There were four microscopes for twenty-five children, and the last time the children had shared materials there had been some trouble.

"We're going to have to do some advance planning today about these microscopes if we're going to avoid the problems we had last time," said Mr. Roberts. "When we tested minerals in our geology unit some of you were arguing about who was going to use what. Today we have four microscopes. If the whole class participates, how many will be in a group?"

"Six in three groups, and seven in the other group?"

"Okay. Now we have a number of things to look at and categorize. How shall we work things?" asked Mr. Roberts.

"Well, when we took turns with the microscopes the other day, everybody rushed me so I couldn't even see what was there," complained Joan.

"Well, some kids take too long. It's not fair," said Bill.

"Why don't we have just one person do all the looking, and the others can do the writing?" suggested Ricky. "Or one person can look and one person can check to make sure, and the others do the other things."

"That's no good—we all want to look. That's the part that's interesting," said Bob.

"Can somebody think of an entirely new solution?" asked Mr. Roberts. "We don't have to divide up by sixes and sevens, you know."

About thirty seconds of silence followed before Bill said, "What do you mean? If we don't do that everybody won't have a chance. There's only four microscopes."

"Yeah, everybody won't have a chance," said Bob.

More silence followed and then Hank burst out, "Oh, I get it. *Everybody* doesn't have to use the stuff today!"

Marcia joined in, "We could have smaller groups and the rest of the class could do something else. Like twelve kids could work today— three to a microscope."

"That's better—let's do that, Mr. Roberts," came from several youngsters. "Then we wouldn't have so much trouble."

"I think that's a good idea, too," agreed Mr. Roberts. "We'll put the four microscopes in the back of the room there, and have three people to an instrument. The rest of us will come up here and review what we've done so far with the background reading. We'll divide up this way. . . ."

ANALYSIS Notice that this case contains the VICS category of silence. How does the teacher's use of this category provide the children with an opportunity for discovery?

There is a tendency for people to be uncomfortable during periods of silence after questions have been asked. Because of this feeling of discomfort, teachers usually fill the gap by asking further questions, by restating the original question, or by giving information or opinion. Sometimes they criticize the class by making such statements as, "You're not thinking," or "You should know the answer." Periods of silence after questions often give pupils needed opportunity to think, to discover new solutions, to reach new insights.

It is likely that Mr. Roberts has decided beforehand that the whole class should not use the microscopes at the same time. However, he presents the problem to the class for discussion in order to provide them with an opportunity to participate in solving a genuine problem. This is quite a different approach from that of the teacher who has planned an activity and then manipulates the class so that they will give "appropriate" responses.

SKILL SESSION   Divide into groups of four or five. Take turns role playing the part of the teacher, and ask questions which because of their nature and phrasing will produce periods of silence before they are answered. Each group might have an observer who will try to identify the characteristics of questions which produce short periods of silence.

Some examples of questions which would be likely to produce thoughtful silence are, "Can you think of some completely new way to approach the problem of —— ?" "What are some of your feelings about —— ?"

For the content of your discussion you might choose any topic which you are currently teaching or studying.

Situation 9A

The eighth grade art class was planning an exhibit of their work for the rest of the Junior High.

"We'll have to think about where we should set up the exhibit," said Miss Wilde, the teacher.

"I think we should use the gym, because that's the biggest place," said Ann.

"But the gym is used every day—and besides, it's too big," objected Tom. "I think the stage of the auditorium would be good. That's usually empty."

"We could have the exhibit after school in the gym," replied Ann.

"But then it could only be for one day," put in Janet.

"Why? We could set it up every day. It won't take long. And it would be fun," persisted Ann. "Let's have it in the gym."

"We'll just have to take a vote," said Miss Wilde. "How many want it in the auditorium? How many in the gym? Well, the gym wins. That means we'll have to have it after school. What do you think of having it just for a day?"

"Naw, we want it for a few days . . . maybe three," said Ann. "We can set it up more than once."

"Well, do the rest of you agree?" asked Miss Wilde. "Two days? Three? Most seem to want it for three days. It will be a lot of work, and I think you may be sorry, but if that's what you want. Now, what kinds of things do you want in the exhibit?"

"I think we should look through the things we've done so far this year and pick the best things," suggested Lisa. "We could vote on what's best."

"I think each person should pick one or two things of his own that he wants," said Janet.

"That's no good—we only want good things in this," said Drew. "Like Vera's work. Her stuff is always good, so we shouldn't have just one or two of her things. And we don't want any stuff that looks crummy."

"But if we only have the things that are good, some kids won't have anything in it, and that's not fair," responded Marion.

"Well, they could help more in setting it up or something," retorted Drew. "We don't want the other kids to laugh at us, do we?"

"Well, who's going to decide what's good and what's bad?" asked Tom. "What if people vote for their friends' stuff, or something like that?"

"We know what's good and bad. It'll be easy to decide," replied Drew.

"What do you think, class?" asked Miss Wilde. "Shall we have something of everyone's or just decide upon the best work? How shall we decide?"

"Vote."

"All right. Let's see the hands of those who want only the best things. Now those who want something from everyone. Well, the best work seems to win. How shall we decide what's best?" aswed Miss Wilde.

"We could go through everybody's folders and the things in the cupboards, and vote," said Drew.

"Then suppose we get started," said Miss Wilde. "This is going to take a lot of time, boys and girls, so we'd better get going."

ANALYSIS   If you analyze this teacher's behavior using the VICS you will find that she neither rejects nor accepts the pupils' statements. She does nothing to clarify, to expand and build upon, or to summarize what the children say. How does she decide upon which suggestions to follow? What do you think of this method of reaching solutions?

The analysis and skill session following situation 9B are relevant to this case.

Situation 9B

Miss Thadwick's eighth grade art class was planning an exhibit of their art work for the rest of the Junior High.

"I think we probably should begin by deciding where in the building we want the exhibit to be held," suggested Miss Thadwick.

"Let's have it in the gym—that's the biggest place," said Sally.

"Naw—that's used all day, and it's too big, anyway," objected John. "I think it should be held on the stage in the auditorium."

"Well, we could have it in the gym after school," said Sally. "And it's not too big."

"But then it could only be for one day. I think it should last longer than that," came from Arlene.

"We could set it up more than once—it could be after school for several days," said Sally.

"Let's see if we can go over the pros and cons of the places mentioned," interjected Miss Thadwick. "The gym is somewhat large, but of course we don't have to use all of it. If we have it there it could only be after school, and if we want it for more than one day we'd have to take it down and put it back up again. And while I don't like to step in too much on your plans, I must tell you from past experience that putting up and taking down is a great deal of work—and not so much fun after the first day."

"Besides," said Kathy, "and this is against the gym, kids would have to stay after school to see it, and maybe they won't want to. And how could we get it up in time? The gym is used last period."

"But the stage is too dark," Kenneth joined in. "We couldn't see the things well. Maybe we could have it right here in the art room. We always have things up anyway, and there's plenty of room. Then the other kids could see it when they come for art, and it would be easy to set up."

"Well, there's a new suggestion," said Miss Thadwick. "Use this room right here. Certainly that would save much carrying back and forth, and I do think that we have a good amount of space. If we wanted to invite the parents we could have them come during our own art time, or I'd be willing to have an afternoon or evening after school, if you like."

"That's the best idea," "I like that," "Good," "Yeah," "Let's have it once at night and we could come too," came from the class.

"How about you, Sally and John—you seemed sold on the other places. What do you think?" asked Miss Thadwick.

"Okay with me," and "I don't care," were the responses.

"Good. I think the choice is a wise one," said Miss Thadwick. "Now, how about the works to be shown? How will we decide upon them?"

"I think we ought to look through what everyone has done and pick out the best things," proposed Sally.

"I think that's a good idea, too. We want the exhibit to have the best work," agreed Marilyn.

"But then some kids might not have anything in the show. And that's not fair," Jean objected.

"Well, an art exhibit is supposed to be the best things," said Marilyn.

"Let's think for a moment about what we want our exhibit to be," suggested Miss Thadwick. "It's true that when we go to a museum we expect to see only outstanding work, but perhaps we might have different goals."

"I still think we should show only the best things," said Marilyn.

"Well, maybe we should show the best things of each person," suggested Tim.

"I think we should have the good things," said Kathy, "but I also think we should all be allowed to show something. This is for us, and also for our parents, so everybody should have something."

"Could we have everybody represented, and also have all the things we think are really outstanding?" asked Miss Thadwick.

"Well, we could have something or at least one thing from everybody," said Tim, "but some people could have more—the kids who are good in art could have more."

"And how will we decide exactly what should be shown?" asked Miss Thadwick.

"Well, each kid could pick the one thing he absolutely wants to be in," continued Tim, "and we could vote on the rest. We could decide what's best after we look."

"Do we need any standards to help us decide what to select?" asked Miss Thadwick.

"We could use some of those things we talk about every so often," said Sally. "You know—line, color, form, texture—those things."

"We could have some examples for each category," said John.

"Fine—and perhaps we could even have sections set up with some discussion notes about these different aspects of our art work. Now," continued Miss Thadwick, "I have some questions about the efficiency of looking through everyone's work as a class. That would be very time-consuming. Anyone think of some other way to speed up the process?"

"Well, everybody could pick out several things they think are their own best things—not just one," suggested Ann. "And then we could choose from those."

"I think that would be wise," commented Miss Thadwick. "And I'd like to suggest that we do this by table. There are six of you at a table, and you can all help each other. While you're doing your selecting, consult your neighbors and see what they think. Remember, sometimes other people think a certain thing is interesting that you might miss. And I'm going to reserve the right to do a little picking myself. Let's get started now. Go through your folders together and through the cupboards, and then we'll see what we come up with. We'll probably just make a beginning today, but right from the start let's see if we can apply our standards when we make selections."

ANALYSIS In both situation 9A and situation 9B there is a great deal of pupil-to-pupil verbal interaction. Notice that this interaction is quite different from that of one pupil speaking after another, but responding directly to the teacher.

Carefully analyze the responses of the teacher in situation 9B to the children's comments. How do these responses differ from those of the teacher in situation 9A?

Miss Wilde, the teacher in situation 9A, seems to feel that a teacher has no responsibility for helping children clarify their ideas and feelings when making plans, while Miss Thadwick, the teacher in situation 9B, evidently conceives of the teacher's role in pupil-teacher planning to be one of summarizer, clarifier, and on occasion, suggester of ideas, Miss Thadwick is, in a sense, actually a participant in the group. Notice also that Miss Thadwick tries for group consensus rather than compromise or majority rule.

SKILL SESSION   Modify the responses of the teacher in situation 9A so that they are more like the responses of the teacher in situation 9B.

CHAPTER 5

Informing

The activity of informing is, of course, an important teaching function. As with all seven teaching activities, informing can be carried out in a number of ways. The teacher may inform pupils by lecturing to them for varying lengths of time, or he may include information and opinion during discussion, or he may, by asking questions or by encouraging pupils to ask questions, help them to inform themselves through their own explorations. Teachers often use texts and other curriculum materials in the process of informing pupils.

When teachers are involved in the informing activity, they often tend to give pupils information first, and then question them about what they have learned. However, it seems wise, at least at times, to involve pupils actively in questioning and searching from the beginning, with the teacher perhaps gradually taking over more of the responsibility for informing as the activity goes on. That is, teachers should think about asking questions first, or encouraging pupils to ask questions first, when informing, instead of asking questions only at the end. In this way pupils are encouraged to think and explore, rather than merely to retrieve what has been already given to them.

If teachers think of pupils as receivers only, then they will carry on the informing activity differently from the way they will if they consider pupils to be givers as well as receivers. But as with all teaching activities, the teacher must be helped to acquire skill. Conviction alone will not help a teacher to vary the informing behavior he uses. It may well be, in the field of education, that teachers modify their convictions about teaching, and become more conservative and controlling in their teaching because they are not helped to acquire the teaching skills necessary to achieve their initial goals. If one cannot behave in accordance with one's convictions, it is natural human behavior to modify those convictions rather than to indulge in self-blame and guilt. In this chapter, as in all the others, it is hoped that you will be helped to acquire skills necessary to carry out your own convictions.

Situation 1A

Miss Jackson had gathered a variety of materials and objects together for use with her kindergarten class, and had placed the materials in six different boxes, one for each table of children.

"There are a lot of things in these boxes, children, and the first thing we're going to do is have Bonnie and Keith come up here for a minute and each pick something out of one of these boxes. Can you each tell us something about what you have picked?"

"Mine is a piece of sandpaper," said Keith.

"And mine's a marble," said Bonnie.

"What else can you tell us about your things?" asked Miss Jackson. "Perhaps you can tell us what they are used for."

"You can play a game with mine," added Bonnie.

"You use mine to smooth things out," said Keith.

"How did you know what these objects were?" asked Miss Jackson.

"I looked at it."

"You used your eyes, didn't you?" commented Miss Jackson. "You can find out about things in other ways, too. How did you know if yours was rough or smooth?"

"Feel it."

"Yes. We have many ways to find out about the things around us. We can look, and we can feel. Can anybody think of other ways we can find out about things—learn what they're like?"

"You could ask somebody?"

"Yes, you can ask somebody else. Let's think of ways to find out all by yourself—without anybody else to tell you. I'll give you some clues. You can use your ———— " and Miss Jackson pointed to her ears.

"Ears." "You can hear things."

"Can you use some other parts of your body to find out about things, besides your ears, and eyes, and your fingers?"

"You could taste it with your mouth."

"And you can use your nose sometimes, like to find out what's on the stove."

"Very good, boys and girls. The things that we've been talking about are called the senses. We have a sense of taste, and a sense of smell, and of hearing, and of sight for seeing, and a sense of touch for feeling. How many is that in all? Let's count. Taste, sight, smell, touch, hearing. Yes—five senses. Now, I'm going to give each table one of these boxes, and I'd like you to put the things that are inside these boxes into different kinds of piles. You can pile them any way you like. For instance, you might put all the wooden things together, or all the big things together. But try to have things in piles with other things which are like them. All right—take about five or ten minutes to do that."

For the next few minutes each group of four children sorted things from the boxes. There were arguments, and some grabbing, but Miss Jackson walked about and helped when necessary. When the children had made a fair amount of progress, she said, "Now, even if you haven't grouped everything, let's stop for a minute and see how you're doing. We'll start over here at this table, and see how these people made their groups. Bessie, would you tell us about some of your things?"

"The marble and the pen is together because they're smooth. And the sandpaper and the piece of rug is together with the pipe cleaner because they're rough."

"Fine. How about this table?"

"We put the marble and the paper clip and the stone and the piece of rug together because they're all small. And we put these things together because they're big. And the others are in-between."

"Very interesting. Did you notice, boys and girls, that the two tables put some of the same things into different groups? One table put the marble in the smooth pile, and the other table put the marble in the little pile. How did they tell that the marble was smooth? Yes, they felt it. And how did the other group tell that their marble was small? They used their sense of sight and looked at it. Good. All right, this table."

"We did soft things and hard things."

When each table had told of its method of grouping, Miss Jackson said, "We certainly grouped our things in different ways. We had big and small, hard and soft, rough and smooth, wood and metal. There are other words we could have used. For instance, we could have said something else instead of saying that we grouped them according to big and small."

"Big and little."

"Yes, we could say that. I can think of another word—size. We can group according to size. Now, suppose we had grouped according to whether these things made a loud or soft noise when we dropped them. What would be another way of saying that?"

"You could say 'noisy' or 'quiet.' "

"Yes, we could say that. I was thinking of just one word, though. Sound. We can group by size, or by sound, or by feel. And there's another word for feel—a big word. Texture. We would look to tell the size—we'd use our sense of sight. And we'd use our sense of hearing for sound, and our sense of touch for texture. And there are many other ways to group. We might have used shape—are the things round, or are they square? Which sense would you use to find that out?"

"Feel."

"Yes, the sense of touch."

"You could look too. You could use sight."

"Very good. To tell about shape you can use your sense of sight or your sense of touch," said Miss Jackson. "Now I'm going to ask you to do some more grouping with the things in your boxes. Get everything back into the boxes, and then I'm going to ask certain tables to do certain things, so you'll have to listen very carefully. Tables one and six will group everything in their boxes according to size. And tables two and five will group everything according to feel, or texture. Tables three and four will pile their things up according to shape."

The children accomplished their tasks quickly, and again Miss Jackson discussed the results with the children. Then she went on, "We've been doing some important work here today. We've been using our senses to find out how things are alike and how they are different. We found that certain things are alike in some ways but different in others. For instance, a marble is smooth like a pen, but different in shape from a pen. If I asked you to take everything that's smooth out of your box, you would take out the marble *and* the pen. But what if I ask you to take out only the things that are shaped round like a ball? . . ."

ANALYSIS   The teacher in this situation uses a variety of techniques to impart information to her class. In addition to the VICS category of giving information, she gives direction, asks broad and narrow questions and accepts pupil responses by building on them. Look through the case and examine the ways in which she uses various VICS categories to inform her class.

When Miss Jackson begins, she does not lecture, but rather she involves the pupils with materials which they examine and group, and she then builds on their experiences with these materials to present further information.

This teacher's assumptions about how to inform children seem to include a belief that if children are allowed to play a part in the dissemination of information they will be more likely to be interested and involved, and more likely to learn and understand the content. The teacher aids the children to actually generate much of the information learned in this lesson. For these children the teacher will not be the sole source of knowledge, and they the receptacles. They are active searchers and participants.

Although the case does not record the conversation of the children in their small groups, they would be using the categories of initiating and responding to each other. The verbal behavior in this case covers a wide range of categories in the VICS. What is one major teacher category that is missing?

SKILL SESSION   Role play a session in which the giving of information is built upon responses received from the class after the teacher's broad questions. The persons who play the role of teacher may select content which they are currently studying or teaching.

Situation 1B

Miss Clark planned to show her kindergarten class a number of materials and objects which were either rough or smooth in texture, and ask them to indicate which was which, have them group the materials in two piles, and finish by making a chart. She began the lesson by asking the children what the words "rough" and "smooth" meant.

"If it's rough, it's bumpy," "Smooth is soft," "Rough is like the sidewalk," "When it's smooth, it's like your skin," were some of the responses.

"Fine," said Miss Clark. "Now, I have many things here in front of me on this tray, and when I call your name, you come up and feel one of them and then tell the class if it's rough or smooth. Then we'll separate them into two different piles, a rough pile and a smooth pile. And when we have the two groups all finished, we're going to paste some of the things up here on this chart I have made. On one side of the chart it says, 'These Are Smooth' and on the other side it says 'These Are Rough.' Now—who will be first? I'm looking for someone who is sitting nicely. Elaine."

Elaine picked up a marble. "This is smooth."

"Yes. Very good. This marble is smooth, and we'll put it here on this side. Now, Frank, you come up."

Frank selected a piece of sandpaper. "This is rough."

"Excellent. We'll put this on the other side. Ann, you may come up and pick."

Ann picked up a paper plate. "This is rough," she said, feeling the fluted edge.

"Rough?" asked Miss Clark in a tone which indicated that she thought otherwise.

"I mean smooth," Ann quickly amended her opinion to conform with that of the teacher.

"Yes, this is smooth. Feel how smooth it is. So we'll put this in the smooth pile. Now, I'm looking for someone to be next. . . ."

ANALYSIS It seems reasonable to assume that superior teachers would have a greater repertoire of verbal behaviors, and be more flexible in their use, than less effective teachers. Notice that the verbal behavior in Miss Clark's classroom includes fewer VICS categories than those used by the teacher in situation 1A. What is the relationship between the different kinds of information acquired by the pupils in the two cases and the difference in range of categories used?

Why do you think the child in this case calls the fluted edge of the paper plate rough? Do you think she understands why the teacher wanted her to say "smooth"? This child seems to have learned that answers are given to please the teacher, and that one does not question the teacher's knowledge—for the teacher is the source of all knowledge.

This teacher might have asked herself an important teaching question when this activity ended: What did the children learn that they did not know before?

SKILL SESSION

1a. Reject the pupil statement, "Smooth is soft," and then give corrective feedback about the difference between softness and smoothness.

b. Accept the pupil statement, "Smooth is soft," and then give corrective feedback about the difference between smoothness and softness.

c. Neither accept nor reject the pupil statement, "Smooth is soft," but lead the pupil to make his own correction about the difference between smoothness and softness.

2*a.* The following exchange takes place in this case: Ann picked up a paper plate. "This is rough," she said, feeling the fluted edge. "Rough?" asked Miss Clark in a tone which indicated that she thought otherwise. "I mean smooth," Ann quickly amended her opinion to conform with that of the teacher. "Yes, this is smooth. Feel how smooth it is. So we'll put this in the smooth pile." Modify this exchange so that the teacher attempts to find out why the pupil calls the plate rough, and so that teacher and child understand why one calls it smooth and the other rough.

Situation 2

"Tomorrow during our work period about six children at a time may finger paint," said Miss Diller to her first grade class. "It will be the first time this year that we will be using finger paint, and everyone might not have a turn, but you will all have a chance within the next few days. I put the jars of finger paint on that shelf over there. Can you tell me what colors we have?"

"Red, yellow, green, black, white," came the responses.

"And do you know, those are the only colors I ordered for the whole year. Last year I ordered many other colors—orange, blue, purple."

"Don't you like the other colors?"

"Yes, I do like the other colors," answered Miss Diller. "But why don't all of you try to find out why I didn't order more colors by asking me questions? See if you can find out the reason."

"Did the principal say you could only have those?"

"No."

"Last year's kids didn't use them right?"

"No."

"Did the store have any other colors?"

"Yes."

"We weren't good, so we can't have all the colors."

"No. And most of the time you are good."

"It's too messy."

"No."

"Maybe you wanted to mix them yourself. Like if you mix red and black you might get another color."

"Yeah—if you mix paint up, you get another color. Is that why?"

"That is why. I thought it would be nice if we mixed the colors we want ourselves. Suppose we want pink. What would we do?" asked Miss Diller.

"Mix yellow and white."

"No, red and white."

"We can find out by mixing those colors. How do you think we could make blue?" asked Miss Diller.

"Yellow and green."

"Yellow and black."

"I want to make orange."

"I want purple."

"All right, let's make some tests right now. I'll get some paper, and we'll do some mixing and see what happens," said Miss Diller as she brought out some finger paint paper.

ANALYSIS   This teacher introduces a unique verbal pattern because she asks the children to ask questions, and she responds to the questions by either saying "yes" or "no." In most classrooms children do not have the opportunity to ask series of questions of the teacher. You may be interested in the inquiry training approach of Suchman, in which he and his colleagues train children to ask questions for the purpose of obtaining information in order to solve problems.[1]

"No" is often a rejecting statement. For instance, if a pupil says "2 and 2 is 3" or "I'm going to take this ball out to the playground," or "Is it time to go home?" or "Isn't it true that Columbus came to the United States?" and the teacher says "no," then the "no" is a rejection. However, "no" may be used to give information. For instance, if a pupil asks, "Shall we wear our sweaters outside today?" or "Was Washington the first capital of the United States?" then the teacher's "no" is not a rejection. In these last two examples the teacher is not saying, "No, you are not demonstrating appropriate behavior, ideas or feeling." He is saying, "The answer to your question is 'no.'" "Yes" as an answer would not mean support

1 J. Richard Suchman, "Inquiry Training: Building Skills for Autonomous Discovery," *Merrill-Palmer Quarterly*, no. 7 (July, 1961), pp. 147–169.

or acceptance, just as "no" does not mean rejection. If the pupil is asking for information rather than seeking confirmation or support, then the "no" response is not likely to be a rejection.

SKILL SESSION

1. Practice asking "yes" or "no" questions which will evoke acceptance or rejection.

2. Practice asking "yes" or "no" questions which will evoke information or opinion.

3. Would the "yes" and "no" answers to the following questions be categorized as acceptance and rejection, or as the giving of information or opinion:

   a. Do you like me?
   b. Do you like my picture?
   c. Was I good today?
   d. Was my report interesting?
   e. Was Washington alive at the same time as Lincoln?

   On what basis did you make your decision?

4. Role play a classroom situation in which the pupils ask a series of "yes" or "no" questions of the teacher in order to obtain information about a topic.

Situation 3A

Mrs. Ragan was introducing her second grade class to simple units of measure, and she began the activity by saying, "Today we're going to learn about liquid measure. Who can tell me what your mother uses when she cooks or bakes at home to measure the amount of milk she wants?"

"Mine uses a cup." "A teaspoon." "A tablespoon."

"Well, I was thinking of a cup, but a cup with a certain name. Who can tell me the name of that cup?" asked Mrs. Ragan.

"A measuring cup."

"Very good. Now, when you go to the store to buy milk, or when the milkman delivers the milk to your home, what kind of bottle is the milk usually in?"

"A milk bottle."

"But what do we call the milk bottle? It has another name."

"You call it a quart bottle," said Karl.

"Good. And how many of those measuring cups fit into a quart? Karl?"

"Four."

"Yes. Some of us aren't listening. Ronnie, turn around and stop fooling with that. You won't know what we're learning about today. All of you, face front and pay attention. Ronnie, what did we just say about how many cups are in a quart?"

"Um. . . ."

"You see what happens when you don't listen. Karl, will you please tell the class again? Yes, there are four cups in a quart. Marion, put that book inside your desk! This class won't know about liquid measure. Now, who knows what half a quart is? Doesn't anyone know anything except Karl? Louise."

"A pint."

"Yes, and now, how many . . . Ronnie, didn't you hear what I said before? What are you fooling with now? Bring it right up here and leave it on my desk. And what's going on over there? Donald, you had better move to the library table. Now I want everyone to pay attention. How many pints are there in a quart? Karl?"

"Two."

"Can anyone figure out how many cups there are in a pint? Row 2! Put your heads down on your desks this minute! How many cups are there in a pint? Karl and Louise seem to be the only two children who are paying attention. Louise?"

"Two."

"Good. Now, class, take your notebooks out and copy what I write on the board. Use your best writing, because this is important and we want to have it in our notebooks so that it is correct."

LIQUID MEASURE

There are four cups in one quart.
There are two cups in one pint.
There are two pints in one quart.

ANALYSIS In this situation we see a pattern which is quite common in many school classrooms: narrow questions, followed by predictable responses, with frequent interjections of rejection of children's behavior. Two children do most of the responding. The teacher accepts the children's correct responses in a perfunctory way —she does not build upon them.

The analysis and skill session which follow situation 3B are related to this situation.

Situation 3B

Mrs. George was going to introduce her second grade class to liquid measure, and she had gathered a variety of quart, pint and gallon bottles, and some measuring cups. She began by asking the children what they thought was meant by the term "liquid measure." The children gave a variety of answers, and it was established that there were some ways for measuring liquids which were different from ways for measuring solids.

Mrs. George displayed the objects she had gathered for this activity and asked the children what they could tell her about the various items.

"That one is a milk bottle," "And it's also a quart bottle. And that's a soda bottle," "That one's a measuring cup—we have one at home," "That one is a pint bottle," "I think the big one is a gallon," came the responses.

"Does anyone know how many of any of these containers are needed to fill any of the other containers?" asked Mrs. George.

"You need two pint bottles to fill the quart." "You need six of the cups to fill the milk bottle." "The soda bottle is the same as the milk bottle," came some answers from the children.

"All right—we'll check some of these answers to make sure. Somebody said that the soda bottle would hold the same amount as the milk bottle. If it does, then what amount would it hold? Yes, a quart," said Mrs. George. "It would be a quart bottle. We have some other jars up here, a mayonnaise jar, and a peanut butter jar, and we'll want to find out how much liquid they hold. How can we find out?"

"We can pour water from the ones we know are quarts and pints."

"Yes. We'll check the ones we aren't sure of by pouring water from the ones that we are sure of. Then we can write the amount of the measure on these labels I have and we can paste them on to the bottles," said Mrs. George.

The class spent some time pouring water and checking the amount held by the bottles they weren't sure of, and when everything was properly labeled, Mrs. George suggested that the class check to find out how many of one measure was required to fill the next largest size. As they did this, she wrote the findings on the board: "Two cups equal one pint. Four cups equal one quart. Two pints equal one quart. Four quarts equal one gallon."

Mrs. George continued from there, "How can we figure out how many pints there are in a gallon?"

"You could pour water in from the pint jar, and you could count how many."

"That would be one good way. Can anyone think of another way?" Mrs. George asked.

"You could say two pints for each quart, and you could make two marks, four times, and then you could add them."

"Why four times? Will you show us what you mean on the board?" asked Mrs. George.

The child went to the board and explained his method, making two tallies for each quart in a gallon, and then showing how he would count up the results.

"So we can see that there is more than one way to solve these problems," commented Mrs. George. "Now, suppose I ask you to tell me how much half a quart is. Can you tell me?"

"Half a quart is a pint."

"How do you know that?"

"Well, there's two pints in a quart. And if you take one away, you have just one left, and that's half. So it's half a quart."

"Good work. Can you come up here and use the flannel board to show us what you did?"

When the child had used the models to show how he had arrived at his answer, Mrs. George asked the class, "Does a quart mean a certain size?"

"Yes."

"No, a quart doesn't mean size—it means . . ." and Mrs. George hesitated.

"It means a certain amount," said one child.

"It always is the same amount, but it can be a different shape, like the soda bottle or the milk bottle. They're both quarts," added another child.

"So measuring containers with the same name will hold the same amount no matter what their shape," said Mrs. George. "A quart always holds a certain amount, and a pint does too. Dorothy and

Alan, would you come up here and figure out as many ways as you can think of to bring me a quart of something? Suppose I told you to bring me a quart of tomato juice from our next-door neighbor. Show me how many different ways you can do it using the things we have here. And the rest of you, while they're doing that, think about what might happen if we didn't have these methods of measuring. By the way, these measures are called standard measures, because they are always the same. A quart in California is the same as a quart in New York. Can you think of any ways that our lives might be different if we didn't have these standard ways of measuring things?"

ANALYSIS   The verbal pattern of the teacher in situation 3A is one in which the same categories tend to recur, while the teacher in situation 3B has a wide range of verbal behaviors. Identify the categories in each situation which one teacher uses and the other does not.

What are some of the reasons why the pupils in Mrs. Ragan's class misbehave, while the pupils in Mrs. George's class are attentive?

Compare some of the probable underlying assumptions of these two teachers about how children acquire information.

SKILL SESSION   Role play one classroom situation in which the teacher attempts to inform the class by asking only narrow questions, and another situation in which the teacher attempts to inform the children about the same topic by using broad questions. The teacher may build upon the pupil responses. The person playing the role of the teacher may select the topic from content he is currently studying or teaching. Compare the two sessions.

Situation 4A

"Open your social studies books to page 42, boys and girls," Mr. Prince directed his fourth grade class. "Today we're going to learn about plows. Phyllis, will you begin reading?"

" 'Of Plows and Plowing[2]

" 'Many tools have been used by man through the ages. Of all the tools, the plow is perhaps the oldest and most useful.' "

2 Taken from *Above the Clouds*, Winston Basic Readers (New York: Holt, Rinehart and Winston, Inc., 1962), p. 42.

"Good. Next person," said Mr. Prince.

" 'Although the oldest of man's many tools, early plows didn't turn up much ground at all. Very poor plows were used in the days before the birth of Christ. Even during the time of Christ, the plows used did not do a very good job. They hardly cut the ground.' "

"Did the first plows cut into the ground well?" asked Mr. Prince.

"No."

"All right. Next reader."

" 'The first plows were little more than large sticks pulled by men. For many hundreds of years the stick plow was the only plow known. Even today, some countries use sticks for plowing.' "

"What were the first plows made of?" inquired Mr. Prince.

"Sticks."

"Yes. Next."

" 'The first real change in plows came in the early 1600's. Dutch farmers, among others, began making wooden moldboard plows. The moldboard lifted and turned the ground, something the early plows could not do. Now a better job of farming could be done.' "

"Why were the moldboard plows better than stick plows?" asked Mr. Prince.

"Because they could lift and turn the ground."

"Good. Next reader. . . ."

ANALYSIS Mr. Prince relies solely upon the text to present the information in this case; and the answers to the extremely narrow questions which he asks are taken directly from the text.

SKILL SESSION Modify Mr. Prince's comments after each pupil response so that he accepts the contribution and gives additional information which is related to the response.

Modify the questions which Mr. Prince asks so that the answers will not be derived directly from the statements which the pupils have just read.

Situation 4B

"In social studies we've been talking about the importance of farming in man's development. Who can mention some of the things we have learned?" asked Mr. Lincoln of his fourth graders.

"Well, if people don't know how to grow their own food, they have to wander around and find things to eat. They can't stay too long in one place."

"And it takes a lot of land for not too many people, because they keep picking the berries and things, and they don't plant anything else. So there couldn't be too many people in those days, because there wasn't enough to eat."

"Good. Now, today, we're going to read some material about the development of one of the most important tools that farmers use—a tool that helps in planting seeds. Anyone have any idea what that might be?" asked Mr. Lincoln.

"A shovel?"

"A plow?"

"A rake?"

"Let's open our books to page 42 and see," directed Mr. Lincoln.

"A plow!" came the answer from the class.

"Yes. Today we're going to read about plows and plowing, and we'll see what effect plows had upon man's ability to grow his own food and grow it in quantity. Sam, would you begin reading?"

" 'Of Plows and Plowing

" 'Many tools have been used by man through the ages. Of all the tools, the plow is perhaps the oldest and most useful.

" 'Although the oldest of man's many tools, early plows didn't turn up much ground at all. Very poor plows were used in the days before the birth of Christ. Even during the time of Christ, the plows used did not do a very good job. They hardly cut into the ground.' "

"All right. Approximately how long ago is the time mentioned in that section?"

"About two thousand years ago."

"Yes. Even before that, though they don't tell us exactly how long before, man began to use plows. Perhaps the exact time isn't known, but let's check on that later. Would you read the next paragraph, Geraldine?"

" 'The first plows were little more than large sticks pulled by men. For many hundreds of years the stick plow was the only plow known. Even today, some countries use sticks for plowing.' "

"That was clear reading, Geraldine. Look at the picture of the stick plow, class. Do you think you could make one?"

"Sure. You just find a stick like that and make the tip sharp with a knife."

"What if you lived in the days when there were no knives?" asked Mr. Lincoln.

"You could use a rock."

"Yes, and that's undoubtedly how stick plows were made. Men were already using rocks as tools, weren't they? Now, how do you think this plow was used, exactly?"

"The person probably took hold of the long end there, and then dragged the pointed tip through the ground."

"What might men have done before they thought to use sticks for plows?" was Mr. Lincoln's next question.

"They could have dug holes with their hands, or they could make that line in the ground with their hands."

"Or they could use a rock."

"Fine. The line you mentioned is called a furrow," explained Mr. Lincoln. "Why is a stick plow an improvement over no tool at all?"

"The stick is stronger than your hand, and it could make a deeper line."

"And you wouldn't have to bend down so much if you're holding the stick, so you could work longer and not be so tired."

"So the stick plow is an extremely useful tool, even though it is so primitive. It's stronger than a man's hands, and you can stand upright and pull it behind you as you walk, instead of having to bend over to make the furrow, so you can cover much more ground. That means that you can plant more seeds, and grow more food. Think for a minute about the kind of person who first thought of using a stick instead of his hands. He had to be an intelligent and imaginative person, and also a person who was looking for better ways of doing things. He wasn't satisfied with the old ways." Mr. Lincoln waited a few moments and then said, "Now, let's read on and find out how plows were improved over the years. Victor, will you read?"

" 'The first real change in plows came in the early. . . .' "

ANALYSIS   Mr. Lincoln ties the information in the text to the children's previous studies, and extends this information by asking questions which require answers that do not stem directly from the material just read. He builds upon the children's answers by summarizing them and by giving new information.

What assumptions do both teachers seem to make about using discussion in the information-presenting procedure?

SKILL SESSION It is possible to inform pupils by using categories other than the VICS category, Giving Information. The information in this case could have been presented in several ways other than through children's reading.

1. Role play a classroom situation in which the teacher presents information to a class by lecturing and then checks the pupils' understanding by asking questions.

2. Role play a session in which the teacher informs a class about a topic by asking narrow questions and making appropriate comments which clarify the information received.

3. Role play a session in which the teacher informs a class about a topic by asking broad questions and making appropriate comments which clarify the information.

Situation 5A

Mr. McCracken read a notice to his fifth graders that he had just received from the principal. "Here's a notice from Mr. Foster. Will everybody listen, please."

> I have received several complaints from parents about the fact that girls are being picked on as they come home from school. Some boys in our school are chasing the girls, teasing them by taking their books, throwing snowballs and otherwise annoying them. This behavior will not be tolerated, and I want it to stop immediately. Any boy who is reported for bothering anyone on the way home from school will be dealt with severely. I trust that this warning will be enough, and that I shall hear no more of this kind of behavior. I expect all of you to behave like ladies and gentlemen.

"Well," said Mr. McCracken, "suppose we take a few minutes to talk about this. I'm not asking any of you to tell tales—but what do you think about boys picking on girls?"

"Oh, they do it all the time. They're always chasing us and everything."

"And they grab our books, too."

"Do the girls ever do anything to make the boys chase them?" asked Mr. McCracken.

"No."

"Not much! They say, 'I bet you can't catch me,' and they start running as soon as they're out of the schoolyard."

"We do not."

"Do you think it's ever fun to chase people—or to be chased?" asked Mr. McCracken.

"No," "Yes," "Sometimes," came the responses.

"There seems to be some disagreement about that," commented Mr. McCracken. "Do you know any running and chasing games?"

"Sure—Cops and Robbers. Hide and Seek. Red Rover."

"And are they fun?"

"Of course. But they're games."

"And isn't that why they're games? Because they're fun? They aren't fun just *because* they're games. I could make up some boring thing and call it a game, but that wouldn't make it fun, would it? So running and chasing must be fun sometimes, because so many games include running and chasing. And I think sometimes running and chasing is fun even if it's not a special game—that is, a game with a special name, like Cops and Robbers. Sometimes just some kids chasing other kids can be fun. But when isn't it fun?" asked Mr. McCracken.

"Well, it's not fun if you don't want to be chased."

"And it's not fun if you're pushed and you fall down, or if they grab your books or throw something at you."

"I agree. It isn't fun to be chased if you don't really want to play. And it certainly isn't fun if anyone is hurt, or if something happens to the things he's carrying, or if clothes are spoiled. Sometimes chasing starts out as a game, but then the ones being chased want to stop the game, because it stops being fun. But it's still fun for the chasers, so they don't want to stop. However, that really isn't fair to the ones being chased. I think that's what's happened to some of you on the way home. Sometimes it's fun and sometimes it isn't. However, this note from Mr. Foster makes it very clear that no more chasing is to take place. And no more of what else?"

"Throwing snowballs."

"Grabbing things."

"Teasing."

"Yes. I think that all of you are old enough to be able to follow Mr. Foster's directions. I certainly hope that you will all walk home peacefully from now on, and I think you can wait that short time until you are home to begin playing. And I mean real play—

not picking on anyone. You all know many games that don't involve hurting anyone else. And by the way, what are some good things to throw snowballs at if you like to throw them?"

"You could throw them at the trees."

"You could throw them up in the air."

"You could make a target."

"You could make a snow fort and then throw them."

"All right. But remember, that's once you're home. You're not to throw any snowballs on the way home. And no more chasing on the way home, either. Save the games for your own yards, and make them games that are fair. Now, let's get back to our reading."

ANALYSIS After reading the principal's notice, Mr. McCracken initiates a discussion with his pupils in order to present further information about and clarification of the notice and the behavior it describes.

Analyze the specific interaction that takes place in this case by referring to the categories in the VICS. Remember that pupils can be informed through the use of several VICS categories. Particularly note how this teacher uses a variety of categories in the process of informing.

If teachers can communicate awareness, understanding, and acceptance of feeling, then children may be in a better position to accept information which involves their feelings. In other words, pupils may be more ready to learn if their feelings are considered.

SKILL SESSION Accept and clarify these expressions of pupil feeling before going on with the activity:

1. Not spelling again!

2. Do we have to write a story today?

3. Can't we just do the examples on this page?

4. I wish I could be in a harder book.

Situation 5B

A notice arrived from the office and Mr. Wilkens read it to his fifth graders. "Here's a notice from Mr. Foster. Will everyone please listen."

I have received several complaints from parents about the fact that girls are being picked on as they come home from school. Some boys in our school are chasing the girls, teasing them by taking their books, throwing snowballs and otherwise annoying them. This behavior will not be tolerated, and I want it to stop immediately. Any boy who is reported for bothering anyone on the way home from school will be dealt with severely. I trust that this warning will be enough, and that I shall hear no more of this kind of behavior. I expect all of you to behave like ladies and gentlemen.

"Well, this note is quite clear, boys and girls. I don't know if any of the boys who have been picking on girls on the way home are in this class or not, and I don't want to know. But if any are in this class, I suggest that they had better stop this behavior at once. Because if I find out that anyone in this class has been chasing anyone else, or throwing snowballs or doing anything else he shouldn't be doing, he's going to be in trouble—and not just with Mr. Foster. Now you had better start behaving yourselves—or else. You've had fair warning, and that should be enough. Let's get back to our books now. Alan, it was your turn to read."

ANALYSIS This teacher reads the information presented in the principal's notice and then, even though there is no pupil talk, he rejects the *possibility* of misbehavior on the part of the class.

What assumptions do these two teachers seem to hold about how children's behavior is changed?

Speculate upon the consequences of these two approaches to presenting the information contained in the principal's notice.

SKILL SESSION Role play a classroom situation in which the teacher reads the following notice from the principal: "It has come to my attention once again that pupils are misbehaving on our school buses. This is the third notice I have sent out to warn you that your behavior must improve. From now on, anyone who is reported twice in one week by a bus monitor for misbehavior will not be allowed to ride the bus for a period of two weeks. I hope that I will not have to write any more notices on this subject, because if I do the punishment will be even more severe."

The teacher will lead a discussion about behavior on the bus in which he will try to help children express and clarify their feelings about behavior on the bus.

Situation 6

Mrs. Ferrara was working with her seventh grade class on making their speech and written work more descriptive and colorful. She began by asking, "Boys and girls, can you describe the tree outside our window?"

"It's green." "It has green leaves." "The trunk is brown." "It's tall."

"Now," said Mrs. Ferrara, "I'm going to write a sentence on the board using the words you have used. 'Outside our window is a tall tree with green leaves and a brown trunk.' Does that describe the tree?"

"Yes."

"Is the sentence an interesting sentence?"

"No."

"Why not?"

"Because it's not interesting. All trees have green leaves and brown trunks."

"And most of them are tall."

"I agree that we don't have a very striking picture of a tree," said Mrs. Ferrara. "There's nothing special about the sentence. The words are just ordinary words. How could we make this sentence more interesting?"

"We could change the words."

"All right. Do you have any suggestions?"

When no one in the class had anything to suggest, Mrs. Ferrara continued. "How about substituting other words for what we have— using synonyms. Try some for tall. Let's make a list on the board."

"High." "Giant." "Enormous."

"Those are good words. Now, I have a book here called a Thesaurus, and I'm going to look up other words for 'tall.' This book is something like a dictionary, but you use it mainly for looking for word substitutes rather than for definitions. You see, I turn to the back of the book where all words are listed in alphabetical order. Then I find the word 'tall,' and there's a number beside it—

206. And then I turn to section 206 in the front of the book. Here it is—I found the number here at the top of the page. Some of the words listed are 'exalted, lofty, gigantic, heaven-touching.' There are others, but I'm just picking out a few. And there is another sort of word substitute mentioned. 'As tall as a maypole, or a steeple.' These are called similes. I'll write that word on the board. Can you think of other similes that begin with 'as tall as'?"

"The Empire State Building." "A skyscraper." "Jack's beanstalk."

"Excellent. Let's get all of these down on the board so that we don't forget them. And now see if you can think of other ways of saying 'green.' "

"As green as an emerald."

"You used a simile—good. Very descriptive. Anyone else think of some very green things that a tree might be likened to?"

"As green as jade." "As green as a cat's eyes."

"Fine. I'm getting all of these down. How about some synonyms for green? Does anyone know any? While we're thinking, Brent, would you try using the Thesaurus to see if that has any synonyms for green? Remember, look in the back first, and find your word, and then look in the front of the book for the number listed beside it. Can anyone think of another word for green? All right, then, let's go on to expand the picture that we have of the tree. Can we say something special about the way in which the leaves are moving, or perhaps about the shape of the trunk? Let's start with synonyms for moving."

"Waving." "Fluttering." "Dancing." "Shaking."

"I found green," said Brent, "and then I had to look under color. I can't pronounce all the words, but there's emerald, verdigris, verdure. . . ."

Mrs. Ferrara walked to Brent's desk and looked at the book. "Most of these words are a little too uncommon. Read this part, Brent. 'Emerald green' and so forth."

"Oh—'emerald green, grass green, apple green, sea green, olive green, bottle green.' "

"That's a little different way of describing things. Instead of saying 'as green as jade' we can say 'jade green.' Or instead of saying 'as tall as a skyscraper' we can say. . . . ?"

"Skyscraper tall."

"Yes. Now I think we have all of our suggestions up on the board. Will everyone please take some paper, and rewrite our original sentence using any combination of words that you like—or using other words if you think of others. Just take a few minutes, and then we'll read some of the results."

When the youngsters had had time enough to compose their sentences, Mrs. Ferrara asked, "Who will volunteer to read? Lydia."

"Outside of our window stands an enormous tree with leaves which flutter and are as green as emeralds."

"All right, we have one example. I'll write on the board as you read. Who else will share with us? Eve."

"Outside of our window is a skyscraper-tall tree with shimmering sea-green leaves, and a wide, wide trunk."

"You have some different words there, Eve. Next? Jess."

"The enormous tree outside of our window is as tall as Jack's beanstalk, and the dancing leaves are as green as a cat's eye."

"Jess talks about dancing leaves in her sentence. Kenny, do you have a sentence?"

When several more children had read their sentences, Mrs. Ferrara said, "I think this is enough for now. Notice that some of these people changed the order of our original sentence, as well as the words. And that's fine. Now—how are these sentences different from our original sentence, 'Outside our window is a tall tree with green leaves and a brown trunk'?"

"The words are better."

"They're more interesting."

"They describe the tree more."

"The words aren't so ordinary. We don't use them all the time."

"Good," said Mrs. Ferrara. "The words are not ones that we use as often, so perhaps we are not tired of them. They are more interesting to us, and in addition the words describe the tree more vividly. We can picture the tree better, perhaps, than we can after reading the first sentence. Now, I'd like us to continue with this, and to become aware of descriptive language in books that we read. For tomorrow I have some good passages from some of our library books, and if you come across any interesting use of words, jot them down to share with us. But before we leave this today, I'd like you to take a new sentence—one that we won't talk about at all—and see if you can make it into a more descriptive sentence. Here it is: 'The boy was afraid and ran down the stairs.' Take a few minutes to play with that sentence and see what you can come up with."

ANALYSIS   In general, this teacher presents information by asking questions which are built upon pupil responses to previous questions, and also by interjecting new information in the course of the discussion. Notice that when Mrs. Ferrara writes the children's sentences on the board she accepts all contributions without praise or criticism. Both praise and criticism often have the effect of cutting off the participation of the present speaker, and of other group members as well. Since every child has a potential role to play in the process of presenting information, teachers should encourage as large a number of pupils to participate as possible. Praise and criticism often say, "That's enough," to the person speaking or they may say to other group members, "Your contribution won't be as good," or "Your contribution will also be criticized." Remember that acceptance and praise are not synonymous.

SKILL SESSION   Role play a classroom session in which the teacher accepts all contributions without using praise or criticism. Choose as a topic anything you wish.

Situation 7

"Why is it that some people are better off— have more money—than others?" asked Mr. Gerald of his ninth grade social studies class.

"Some people have better jobs than others, and they make more money."

"Some people are smarter than other people, so they can get better jobs."

"A lot of people who are rich had the money left to them by their parents."

"Some people are lazy and they are the poor ones, and others work hard, and they are better off."

"Some people might save their money and invest it, and others just spend everything they make, and they never get anywhere."

"The more education you have the more chance you have to be well off, but if you don't go far in school, or if you go to schools that aren't good, you'll probably be poor."

"We seem to be saying," said Mr. Gerald, "that there are a variety of reasons for the fact that different people have different amounts of wealth. The amount of education, the degree of intelligence, the opportunities you have, the financial condition of your parents, how industrious you are—all these might have an effect on how well off a person is. Let's look at one of these for a moment—industriousness. That is, how hard you work. Will hard work necessarily make you better off?"

"Of course, if you really work hard, you'll get someplace."

"It depends on what you mean by hard work. Somebody who digs ditches works hard, but he doesn't make as much money as a banker, say."

"So the amount of physical effort you exert doesn't necessarily have anything to do with how much money you make. How about the number of hours you work? If you work longer hours will you make more money?" asked Mr. Gerald.

"Well, I know that in poor countries, like in Asia, they work very hard and long hours, but they're poor. But in this country many people work short hours and it isn't hard work physically, and they're well off."

"Is there a greater chance for people to be better off in some countries than in others?" came Mr. Gerald's next question.

"Sure. There's more chance to be well off here than in India."

"Why is that?" inquired Mr. Gerald.

"Because there's more industries here, so there's more chance of getting a job."

"People are better off, so there's more chance that your parents will be able to help you."

"More people can go to school and. . . ."

ANALYSIS   Is there any instance in this situation of the teacher's using the VICS category, Giving Information. What two kinds of teacher verbal behavior does Mr. Gerald use in this case? Explain how information is presented in the case.

SKILL SESSION   In order to consciously select the verbal behavior which you wish to use in your teaching, you must practice using a variety of teacher statements. Each teacher statement in this case may be modified so that it will fall into a different VICS category. Read each teacher statement and change it so that it falls into two or three other VICS categories.

CHAPTER 6

Leading Discussion

Leading discussion can, of course, be carried on as part of any of the six other teaching functions, but in this book a separate chapter is devoted to it because it can be defined as a teaching activity apart from the other six, and also because it is such an important part of teaching. Again, leading a discussion well is an acquired skill. One must learn to listen, to accept, to encourage pupil-initiated talk, to build on the ideas of others and to allow cross-conversation between pupils.

Most teachers would like to engage their classes in discussions which involve many pupils, and yet so often classrooms are dominated by the talk of the teacher and a few verbal youngsters who perhaps have learned to respond in ways which teachers approve, or who are not easily daunted, or who have strong drives to participate and be recognized. A teacher must *learn* to recognize and avoid subtle rejections which discourage pupil talk.

Many college students have had such unfortunate experiences in their school backgrounds that they hardly speak in class throughout their college careers. And, of course, college teachers are no different from other teachers in their need to acquire skill in leading discussion. If college students, who presumably have had fairly successful school careers, are hesitant about participating in group discussion, one can imagine how youngsters whose school careers were discouraging feel about speaking up in a group.

The situations presented in this section are included because of their possibilities for helping the reader develop his discussion-leading skills—skills which are so important in the classroom.

Situation 1

Mrs. Fraser asked her first grade class to draw pictures of the people who lived with them, and when the pictures were drawn the children spent some time looking at each other's work and talking about their families.

"Do any of the people in your families work at jobs outside the home?" asked Mrs. Fraser.

"My mother does," "So does mine," "My father works," "My grandmother's got a job," were some of the responses.

"Do you know what kind of work they do—what their jobs are?" Mrs. Fraser asked.

"I don't know what my father does. I think he goes to the shop."

"My mother cleans houses for people."

"I don't know where my mother works, but she goes out to work when I go to school."

"Nobody works in my house. Me and my brother go to school and my little sister, she stays home and my mother stays home too."

"How many of you have someone in your family who stays home most of the day—takes care of the house and the younger children if there are any?" was Mrs. Fraser's next question.

"My mother just stays home."

"My father, he stays home. My mother goes to work and she don't get home till after supper. My father takes care of the kids."

"My father don't do nothin' in the house. He just works outside."

"My mother works and my grandmother takes care of the kids."

"Why is it that some people in families have jobs?" asked Mrs. Fraser.

"Well, if you have a job you make money."

"You get a pay."

"Yeah, my father always brings home his pay."

"My mother makes a lot of money because she works in the hospital."

"My mother says she's gonna go to work next year when all us kids is in school."

"Well, we've heard that very often someone in the family goes outside to work, in order to make money. But why do we need money?" queried Mrs. Fraser.

"To get the food."

"You gotta pay for clothes and shoes and things like that."

"Yeah, and you gotta give money to the man if you want something like candy or ice cream."

"So we need money to buy food and clothes and many other things. We need to have money to pay for the places we live in. And people work at all kinds of different jobs so that they can earn money to pay for the things that they need. Sometimes mothers work, or fathers, or grandmothers. Sometimes no one in the family is able to work. Sometimes people can't find a job. Then the government usually gives the family enough money to buy food and clothes and pay the rent. Remember, we talked about the government yesterday," Mrs. Fraser reminded the class. "Do you know where the government gets its money?"

"They make money in factories. I saw it on TV."

"Yeah, and then they give it to people."

"Well, they do make money; that is, they print money, but it isn't quite as simple as just making the money and handing it out to people. The money has to be paid for. And everybody pays some money to the government by paying taxes. We give money, called taxes, to the government so the government will have extra money for people who need it; and to build roads and many other things. You might pay taxes yourself, for instance, if you buy a box of candy. Some of the money goes to the storekeeper, some goes to the people who make the candy, and a little extra goes to the government so they will have it to give to some families and for all the other things that the government pays for. Do you know who pays me?"

"Do you work?"

"Well, yes, I get paid for being a teacher. The city government pays me for working as a teacher."

"You get paid for being a teacher!"

"I wanna be a teacher when I grow up."

"I wanna be a truck driver."

"Don't be a truck driver, be a astronaut."

"Me too."

"I'm gonna be a nurse like my sister."

"For homework tonight," said Mrs. Fraser, "let's all think about what we'd like to work at when we grow up, and we'll talk about that tomorrow. Also, for homework I'd like you to find out what jobs the people in your families have. Ask them about what they do at work. And tomorrow we'll talk more about jobs and money."

ANALYSIS This teacher asks a series of related questions. Identify which of these questions grow directly from the children's comments and which the teacher uses to open an entirely new line of thought.

There is a good deal of pupil participation in this case. Are the pupils responding to each other, or to the teacher, in most instances? Identify the pupil-initiated statements in this discussion.

One reason for the great amount of pupil participation is that the teacher allows several children to talk before she speaks again. The usual classroom pattern is for the teacher to talk after each child speaks.

SKILL SESSION Role play a situation in which the person acting as teacher does not speak, after his initial statement, until at least two pupils have spoken. This means that the teacher must wait after each pupil speaks in order to encourage other pupils to speak. In an actual classroom, the teacher might need to begin this practice by telling the pupils of the procedure he will follow. In the role playing you might choose as your topic any subject which you are currently teaching or studying.

Situation 2

Miss Killian's second grade class was having news time, and Randy was reporting on his trip to the state fair. He had a newspaper picture of some of the booths and exhibits.

"Then we saw this big bull that won first prize. . . ."

"I saw that too—that was good!" said Steve.

"Did you raise your hand, Steve?" asked Miss Killian.

"And then," Randy continued, "we walked around and we saw this booth here in this picture, and then we went to the picnic area and we had our lunch and we had sandwiches and I had a coke and my sister had orange soda and we had cake. And then we went back to the fair, and I didn't want to. . . ."

"Lila and Jean! You're not being polite," admonished Miss Killian. "We listened to you when you had your turn, and now you should be willing to listen to Randy."

"Well, I didn't want to go back to the animal part, but we had to 'cause that's where my father wanted to go. We saw some chickens, and some goats, and some . . . uh. . . ."

"Cindy, Danny and Tommy! You know we don't talk during news time unless we raise our hands and the speaker calls on us. Go on, Randy," directed Miss Killian.

"Well, we saw some pigs and some goats and uh . . . I can't remember. Any comments?" asked Randy of the rest of the class.

"He talked too long," "He shouldn't tell us all the animals. We know that part," "He should have told more about the rides," were some of the comments.

"All right, sit down, Randy," said Miss Killian. "Next person? Laura."

"Well we went to the fair, too, on Sunday, and we had lots of fun. We saw the cows and the horses, and we went on some rides and we had ice cream. . . ."

"Mary and Randy are not being polite. Randy, we just listened to you tell your news. Now it's your turn to listen politely. Go on, Laura."

ANALYSIS   Describe the talk in this situation by referring to the categories in the VICS. How many of the teacher's comments are related to the pupils' topics? What part does the teacher seem to play in this discussion?
Many teachers think of "show and tell" time, or sharing time, or news time, as periods for encouraging discussion. Often, however, there is little or no real discussion during these times, and teachers find themselves spending an inordinate amount of time reprimanding pupils who are misbehaving. How could the teacher in this case help children respond to each other's comments, and how could she participate in the content of the discussion so that children would be more inclined to listen to each other?

SKILL SESSION   Role play a sharing time or news time in a classroom, and have the person playing the part of the teacher encourage pupils to build on other pupil's ideas. Such statements as, "Will someone comment on what Bill said?" or "Would someone like to develop that idea further?" or "Did anything like that ever happen to anyone else?" are helpful. When pupil's initiate talk they should try to speak to another pupil rather than to the teacher.

Situation 3

The second graders were discussing the kinds of food they had eaten for Thanksgiving, and were comparing them to the foods eaten on the first Thanksgiving.

"What did your family eat, Jerry?" asked Miss Olney as she selected from the multitude of waving arms.

"We had turkey just like the Pilgrims, and me and my cousins ate at a separate table, and we just kept laughing all the time," replied Jerry. The instant he finished, hands shot up around the classroom as everyone wanted to share his experiences.

"You know, children," said Miss Olney, "everyone is anxious to tell about his Thanksgiving, but we just don't have time to listen to each person. Besides, after awhile we get tired of listening when too many people have a turn. So I have an idea. Each of you can tell your neighbor about your Thanksgiving, and then everyone will have a turn. I'll walk around and listen to everyone. Pull your chairs close to the person next to you, starting with the row near the window. We'll try to speak very quietly, so that everyone can hear. Okay—let's begin moving."

ANALYSIS   This teacher knows how important it is for each child to have a chance to tell about his experiences in a discussion. One way of solving the time problem and the problem of restlessness, and yet giving everyone a chance to share his experiences or ideas or feelings, is to break the class into groups. The younger the children, the smaller the groups will probably be. And when teachers first begin using discussion groups, they may feel more secure in setting up very small groups.

SKILL SESSION   Hold a total group discussion for about five minutes on the topic, "Where I would like to spend my next vacation." Then divide the class into groups of two or three, and continue the same discussion for about five minutes more. Next come back to the large group and discuss the same topic for about five more minutes. Analyze the ways in which the second total group discussion differs from the first. When was it easier to listen to what other group members had to say? When were you more involved in the large group discussion? What implications does this have in terms of involving the largest number of children in the total group discussion? What are the values of small group discussion apart from the contribution this can make to the total group discussion?

Situation 4

Miss Fisher was talking to her third grade class. "Do you remember yesterday we talked about the fact that people might see exactly the same thing, but see it differently—or feel differently about what they see? When we acted out some 'Finders Keepers, Losers Weepers' games, we found that we feel sad if we lose the ball, but happy if we find the ball. Well, today we're going to do something else like that. We're going to look at a story with the same happenings, but through the eyes of different characters in the story. We're going to take a familiar story and tell it over again from the point of view of another character. I thought we'd start with *Sleeping Beauty*. Let's hear it first the way we always do, and then we'll think about how the same story might have been told from the point of view of the thirteenth wise woman—the one who wasn't invited to the feast. Who would like to tell us the story as we usually hear it? Harriet?"

When Harriet had finished telling the story Miss Fisher said, "You kept us all interested, Harriet. Now, we're going to take five or ten minutes to talk about how the thirteenth wise woman might have told the story from her point of view. We'll divide into groups of three, as we usually do, and exchange ideas."

As the children talked with each other in their small groups, Miss Fisher moved from group to group listening and occasionally making a suggestion. When the children had had enough opportunity to pool their ideas, Miss Fisher asked, "Which group would like to be first?"

"We have a good one, Miss Fisher," said Walter.

"All right, Walter, why don't you tell us your group's story."

"Once upon a time," began Walter, "there was a king and queen and they finally had a baby princess, and they were so happy they decided to have a big feast to celebrate. There were thirteen wise women in the kingdom, and the king wanted to invite all of them, but he had only twelve golden plates for them to eat out of, so he didn't invite one wise woman. Well, when the one who was left out heard about the good party they were going to have, she cried and cried. She was a friend of the king, and she wanted to go to the party too. 'I don't care if I don't have a gold plate to eat out of, I just want to go to the party. I think I'll go anyway.' So she went, but they wouldn't let her in because she wasn't invited, even when she said who she was and that she didn't care what kind of plate she had. So then she was really mad. 'What did I ever do to the king to make him mean to me? Nothing! Well, I'll show him. He can't be mean to me—I'll be mean to him, too.' And she was so mad she pushed the guard away and ran into the room where the feast was. When she saw the king, she yelled, 'Your daughter will prick her finger on a spinning needle when she's fifteen, and she'll die.' And that's our story," finished Walter.

"What do you think about that, class?" asked Miss Fisher.

"That was good," was the general opinion.

"I thought so too," agreed Miss Fisher. "Did you like the thirteenth wise woman better in Walter's story than you usually do when you hear it? Why is that?"

"Because I felt sorry for her," "The king should have invited her anyway," "The king was mean," "The wise woman was good, so the king should have been nice to her," were some of the responses.

"Even though this was only a story, we can see that the same happenings can look quite different to different people. Just as the person who loses the ball doesn't think it's fair for the one who finds it to keep it; the one who finds it thinks the ball should be his, because he found it. The same situation, but different views. Can you think of some other stories we can tell from the point of view of another character?" asked Miss Fisher.

"*Jack and the Beanstalk* by the giant," "The stepsister in *Cinderella*," "The wolf in *Red Riding Hood*."

"A good beginning. Try thinking about others, and we'll go on with this tomorrow, because I see that we're running out of time now. By the way, the stories don't have to be the old ones. How about Templeton the rat in *Charlotte's Web*?"

"Tell me," continued Miss Fisher, "do you ever find that you and your brothers and sisters sometimes have different versions of the same events?"

"*Yes!* My brother always picks on me, and then he tells my mother that it's my fault."

"Yeah—my brother picks on me too, and then my mother blames us both, even when it isn't my fault. It's not fair."

"My sister and me always play together, and then we fight, and we always say it's the other one's fault, but my mother always says, 'Then don't play together.' "

"I have to watch my little brother sometimes, and whenever he cries my mother blames me, and I didn't even do anything."

"Do you think that your brothers and sisters would agree with your versions of the stories you just told?" asked Miss Fisher.

"Naw—because we think we're right and they think they're right."

"Then that's another example of two people telling about the same event from different points of view. Well—we'll go on with this tomorrow . . . and you be thinking about other stories we can tell."

ANALYSIS   Describe and discuss the talk in this situation by referring to the categories in the VICS.

SKILL SESSION   One of the most important skills necessary for participating effectively in group discussion is the skill of listening. Divide into groups of three, with two people being discussants and the third person acting as judge. Select a topic which will allow disagreement between the discussants. (The topic may come from any field such as politics, religion, mutual acquaintances, or education. If there is difficulty in deciding upon differences of opinion, just arbitrarily take opposite sides on some issue.)

In order to practice listening, each discussant must summarize or reflect what his partner has just said before he can go on to present his own views. If he does this successfully, then the discussion continues. If he fails, the judge will direct him to backtrack.

Before you begin, study the following examples:

Example 1:

Discussant X	I think American education is inferior to European education.
Discussant Y	So you think European schools are better than ours. Well, I disagree. Our country is the greatest in the world.
Discussant X	That's not relevant to our discussion.
Judge	You forgot to summarize what your partner said.
Discussant X	You disagree with my point of view because you think that our country is the greatest in the world. But I

don't think that's relevant. A country can be great and
not have a great school system.

Example 2:

Discussant X I think American education is inferior to European
education.
Discussant Y You think Europeans are better than we are.
Judge You did not correctly reflect what your partner said.
Discussant Y You think American education isn't as good as European education. Well, I don't agree. Everybody knows
we're more democratic than they are.

Example 3:

Discussant X I think American education is inferior to European
education.
Discussant Y I disagree with you that American schools aren't as
good.
Judge You shouldn't present your point of view until you
objectively reflect your partner's point of view.

In Example 1, the error is one of omission, in Example 2, one of
distortion, and in Example 3, the error is one of inserting one's own
opinion into the summary.

Situation 5A

"Now that you've had time to finish this
story," said Mrs. Rider to one of her fourth grade reading groups,
"we'll discuss what you've been reading. What was the name of the
boy in this story?"

"Whitey."

"All right, who can tell me where he lived and what he did?"

"He lived on a ranch with his uncle, and he was a cowboy."

"Good. Do you remember what his brand was, and how many
cattle he had?"

"His brand was 101, and he had two calves."

"Who can help with that answer?" asked Mrs. Rider.

"His brand was the Rattlesnake brand."

"That's right. His brand was the Rattlesnake, and he hoped that someday it would be as well known as 101. What was it that Whitey wanted at the beginning of the story and how did he plan to get it?"

"He wanted a new saddle, and he was going to sell his calves to get it."

"And did he sell his cattle?"

"No, they were killed by the rustlers."

"Good. Did he ever get the new saddle?"

"Yes."

"How?"

"He helped to catch the rustlers and so he got a new saddle for that."

"Good. Do you think he was proud of that saddle?"

"Yes."

"Did you like this story?"

"Yes."

"Fine. Now we have time to read the story aloud. Will you begin, Tim?"

ANALYSIS You will notice that this teacher asks only narrow questions which require short, predictable responses. We have spoken earlier of the fact that teachers often seem to be uncomfortable with classroom situations that they do not control rather tightly. Most teachers structure discussions in their classrooms so that there is little in the way of unpredictable response, pupil-initiated talk to the teacher, or pupil-to-pupil talk. Even though many teachers express the desire to have open discussions with wide pupil participation, they do not seem to possess the necessary skills. However, these skills can be learned.

SKILL SESSION Modify the questions which the teacher asks in this case so that they require more unpredictable responses. Then role play a classroom situation using those questions, and after each pupil response pause until another pupil comments; or make comments that will encourage other pupils to talk. Comments such as, "That's one idea, now what are some others?" or "What do the rest of you think of that?" or "Would anyone else like to comment on what Jack said?" are helpful.

Situation 5B

"You've all had time to finish the story assigned for today," said Mrs. Garber to one of her fourth grade reading groups, "so let's take some time to discuss it."

"I wish I was Whitey and lived on a ranch. He was lucky."

"Yeah. He was a real cowboy, and he was only the same age as us."

"What do you mean by 'real' cowboy?" asked Mrs. Garber.

"Well, he had his own horse, and he wore cowboy clothes."

"And he worked like the cowboys do. He roped cattle and he rode around the ranch."

"He didn't rope cattle like at a roundup. All he did was use his rope to pull a calf out of the mud."

"Do you think that would be part of the job of a cowboy?" Mrs. Garber inquired.

"Sure."

"I saw a show on TV where the rustlers got the cattle. But they didn't take the meat like in this story and leave the hides. They took the cattle with them."

"Yeah, I saw a show like that. The bad guys were rustlers."

"How did the rustlers look in this story?" asked Mrs. Garber.

"Well, they were just ordinary. They didn't look like bad guys."

"Would you read the part of the story that tells about that, Sandy?" Mrs. Garber requested.

Sandy found the place and read, " 'They didn't look like the bad men Whitey had imagined. They weren't wearing guns, and they didn't talk big to the sheriff. They wore overalls, like homesteaders. One even had on a straw hat and plow shoes. Whitey was mighty disgusted with them.' " [1]

"Why was Whitey disgusted with them?" was the next question.

"Because they looked like ordinary people instead of like bad men."

"Why would that matter?" pursued Mrs. Garber.

"Well, it would have been more fun for Whitey if they looked like the bad guys we see on TV. He probably read some stories about rustlers and then he was disappointed."

"So it might have been more exciting to him if the rustlers had

[1] "Whitey Steers Ahead," *Above the Clouds*, Winston Basic Readers (New York: Holt, Rinehart and Winston, Inc., 1962), p. 196.

guns in their holsters and if they sounded tough. Probably most thieves just look like ordinary people, though," commented Mrs. Garber. "How can you figure out how much reward money Whitey received for his part in catching the rustlers?"

"You have to divide six into fifty, because there was fifty dollars and it had to be shared by six people."

"How much did that amount to, then?"

"About eight dollars and something—so Whitey couldn't buy a saddle."

"I've got eight dollars saved up for a bike."

"Where did you get the money to save?" asked Mrs. Garber.

"Well, I get a quarter for an allowance, and if I do some extra things for my mother sometimes I get paid."

"This summer we sold lemonade and we made some money. But we spent it."

"Do you think Whitey's uncle might give him any more calves of his own, so that he could try again to earn some money?" inquired Mrs. Garber.

"He doesn't need the money anymore. Because the cattlemen gave him a saddle."

"Yeah, but the story said he had old boots and an old hat, so he could still have things to buy."

"Or he could save up to buy his own ranch when he's grown up."

"Why do you think," Mrs. Garber went on, "that Whitey's uncle said not to bother the rustlers on the way into the range?"

"Well, they had to catch them with the meat—otherwise they couldn't really prove that they were thieves."

"Yeah—they had to catch them with the goods."

"What does that mean—the 'goods'?" Mrs. Garber asked.

"The things you steal are the goods."

"What do you think the sheriff meant when he said, 'We'll put these men to soak in the cooler for a spell'?" asked Mrs. Garber.

"The cooler's the jail. He was going to put them in jail."

"What's the reason for having jails," was Mrs. Garber's next question.

"If you do something bad you can go to jail. Like these rustlers took cattle that wasn't theirs, so they had to be locked up."

"You have to have a jail to keep the bad people away from the other people."

"I know somebody who went to jail. A man on our street took some money from the place where he worked, so they sent him to jail."

"All right. That's all the time we have today," said Mrs. Garber. "For your seatwork tomorrow I'm going to assign you to groups so that you can make up a script for a TV show about a cowboy or cowgirl on a ranch. For homework tonight you can think of ideas for your script. Now let's quietly take our chairs back to our places."

ANALYSIS   The questions asked by the teacher in this situation are less restrictive than those asked by the teacher in situation 5A. What else accounts for the difference in interaction patterns in the two situations?

The VICS provides two important approaches to analyzing verbal behavior. The *type of talk* can be looked at, and also the *length of time* that each type of talk extends can be examined. Both are important and are discussed further in the Appendix.

SKILL SESSION   Using the Gallagher and Aschner categories (see Chapter 3, situation 3), change Mrs. Garber's questions so that each question falls into some other category. That is, if the question is convergent, try to modify it so that it becomes divergent, or evaluative, or cognitive memory.

Situation 6

Mr. Farnum's fourth grade class had just viewed a science program on TV, and the television teacher had closed the program with some questions and several suggestions for further activities. The program had been about seasonal changes.

"Now let's break up into groups of four as we decided beforehand," said Mr. Farnum when the program ended, "and carry out the activities we just heard about. You all have materials to work with, so you can get started right away, and I'll be here if you need me."

As one of the groups of children gathered around the desks which had been pushed together, Larry said, "Come on, let's get going. Let's do the chalk line and flashlight thing first."

"Okay, I'll draw the line," suggested Donald.

"I've got the flashlight," came from Beverly.

"Remember, Mr. Farnum said everybody should have a chance. Last time I only did the writing," complained Mary, "so somebody else will have to do that this time. I want the flashlight."

"No—you take the chalk. I want the flashlight," Beverly insisted.

"We can all have a chance. Why doesn't Mary draw the line," suggested Larry, "and then everybody can have a chance with the flashlight. You go first, Bev."

Mary drew a line on a paper on the floor, and Beverly held the flashlight directly over the line while Mary drew a circle around the spot of light. Beverly then slanted the flashlight so that the light made a larger circle.

"Hey, look at the difference in the size of the circles!" exclaimed Donald. "Gimme the flashlight."

"Okay, and I'll draw your circles on some paper," said Larry.

"And then it's my turn for the flashlight, don't forget," reminded Mary.

"Who's writing down what we find?" asked Beverly.

"Not me. I'm going up to get one of the globes for the next part," said Mary.

"I'll write. All you have to do is fill in this form he gave us," said Larry.

"You can see why it's hotter in summer. That's pretty good!" commented Donald.

"I don't see why," said Beverly.

"Because it makes more heat—it's not spread out so much, so it's hotter. It's like concentrated or something."

"That's good. I'll write that down. How do you spell 'concentrated'?" asked Larry.

"C-o-n-s-e-n-t-r-a-t-e-d."

"Okay. Did everybody have a chance with the flashlight? Then we can do the globe experiment."

ANALYSIS   How does the interaction in this situation differ from that in other situations in the book?

Which VICS categories describe the interaction in this situation?

Categorize the interaction between the children by adapting the VICS categories 1 through 6 to pupil talk.

SKILL SESSION   Describe some verbal behaviors which a teacher might use if he were present with this group. When might he make comments, and what kinds of comments would they be?

Discuss ways in which the pupils might react to various teacher comments.

Situation 7A

"Yesterday we said that today we'd begin discussing the important products and industries of our state," Mr. Olsen reminded his fifth grade class. "First of all, why is it that certain states have different products and industries from others?"

"Well—some states might not have any good farm land, so they can't grow some things."

"And they have different climates. Like in the south they can grow cotton, but they can't in the north."

"And sometimes it could be the size. A small state might not have enough room for something like a big ranch with cattle and stuff."

"So," said Mr. Olsen, "the natural resources of the state, the climate, the size—these are important in determining what a state can produce. The amount of rainfall, the waterways for transportation, whether or not there are mountains, and so forth. You mentioned products that can be raised or grown, like cotton and cattle. What about industries?"

There was no response from the class, so Mr. Olsen continued, "Would means of transportation have anything to do with industries?"

"Yes. If a state has good transportation, then they can make things and send them to other states."

"And also they could get raw materials more easily if there's good transportation. Things could be brought to the cities."

"Why is it that factories are usually found in the city?" asked Mr. Olsen.

"Because there isn't room where the farms or the mines are. The country has the raw materials and the city has manufacturing."

"Where are more workers needed?" continued Mr. Olsen, "in factories or on the farms?"

"In the factories—so that's why they are in cities."

"Yes, although machines are taking over the jobs of men more and more in both country and city, we still usually find that more men are needed to work in industries than are needed on farms or in mines. Now, let's see if we can begin to list the most important products and industries in our state, and at the same time think about why they are important. I have a topographical map here, and as we talk let's look at this map to see if that can help us to understand why particular products and industries are found in our state."

"Well, we have big paper mills in our state—they're an important industry. And we probably have them because we have so many forests in the north."

"And the mills are in Center City because there's rivers to get the lumber there. And then they have a lot of roads and railroads to take the paper they make out to the rest of the country."

"Do you think," asked Mr. Olsen, "that Center City has a large population because people came there to work in the mills, or are the mills there because there were people settled there already? And look at where Center City is located on this map. Could this big paper manufacturing center have been located just as well in some other part of the state?"

ANALYSIS   Analyze the talk in this situation by referring to the categories in the VICS.

SKILL SESSION   How might this teacher cover the same information by encouraging the children to ask questions of each other and of the teacher? The teacher's first few questions will be particularly important.

Situation 7B

"All right, boys and girls, today's subject in the study of our state is products and industries," said Mr. Innes to his fifth grade class. "Now, who knows some of the things that are manufactured in our state?"

"Steel."

"Right."

"Machines."

"Good."

"Paper."

"Yes."

"Furniture."

"Yes."

"Do we find manufacturing mostly in the southern part of the state or in the north?"

"The south."

"Yes. And what do we find more of in the north?"

"Farming and forests."

"Right. Now," continued Mr. Innes, "what are some of the important products grown in our state?"

"Wheat."

"Yes."

"Corn."

"Good. And there are other things which are important—not plants, but we find them in the south."

"Livestock."

"Fine. I see that you've read the paragraphs in our book carefully," Mr. Innes commended the class. "Now let's move on to climate."

ANALYSIS   Compare the pattern of teacher questions and teacher responses to pupil comments in situations 7A and 7B. Notice that all pupil talk in situation 7B comes in one- or two-word statements. What does Mr. Innes, the teacher in situation 7B, do that produces these short responses? Why does Mr. Olsen, the teacher in situation 7A, get longer responses?

SKILL SESSION   Modify the teacher talk in situation 7B so that pupils' answers are longer and more complete, and so that pupil talk covers a broader range of categories.

Situation 8

"Yesterday," said Mrs. Washington to her sixth grade class, "we were talking about the discovery of the new world, and the search for trade routes to India. After the discovery of the new world it was some time before settlers arrived here to stay, rather than just explore. The settlers were people who moved away from Europe for good—they didn't plan to return. Now let's think about why people move about on this earth of ours. Why doesn't everyone just stay where he is born?"

"Maybe they don't like it where they are."

"They might not be able to find a job."

"Somebody might be picking on them."

"Maybe they just want to live in a new place."

"How many of you have moved from a different city?" asked Mrs. Washington. "Quite a few, I see. Do you know why your families moved?"

"My father didn't have no job on the farm no more."

"The place where my father worked was closed down, so we had to move."

"We came here to live with my grandmother."

"We moved so's we could be near the hospital, because my brother has to go every week or so."

"I don't know why we moved. I was little then."

"And how many of you have moved to a different house or apartment right here in our city?" asked Mrs. Washington. "A large number. Do you know why you moved?"

"Our apartment was too small for all us kids, so we had to get another one."

"They built a new building where we used to live, so we had to move."

"My mother didn't like the other school where I went."

"The people we lived with, they said we had to move out."

"So you moved for a variety of reasons," said Mrs. Washington. "Sometimes it was because of jobs, or because more room was needed by your families, or they wanted to be in a different place, or they couldn't stay where they were anymore. Now, let's think back to the early settlers. Do you know any reasons why they left their homes in Europe to come to this strange new land?"

"They probably didn't have no jobs where they used to be."

"I know a reason—they didn't like the king."

"Yeah, and they was afraid to go to the church they wanted."

"Maybe they came because it was too crowded where they live. Like from Puerto Rico. There ain't enough jobs there."

"So people are still moving about on the earth, often in search of better things. People move from country to country and from state to state, and even from street to street. And the reasons are often the same today as they were when the early settlers came here looking for political freedom or religious freedom, or because they wanted better lives for themselves and their children. They didn't want certain people to tell them how they had to think and they wanted a chance to improve themselves. Many of the reasons why people move are the same today as they were many years ago."

"Does everyone move willingly?" Mrs. Washington continued. "Do people always move because they want to?"

"No. We didn't want to move, but my father said we had to because of his job."

"All right. And I can think of two large groups of people in this country who did not want to move. One group was brought here by force, and the other group was already here, but was pushed out. Their land was taken away and they were moved to other places against their will. Who am I talking about? . . . Yes, the Negroes and the Indians. Now your assignment for tonight is to think about why these two groups were treated as they were, and what has happened to them since. Tomorrow we'll go on with this topic. I'll write the two questions on the board and you copy them for your homework thinking."

ANALYSIS   This teacher has a good bit of pupil participation, but the children respond to the teacher in turn, for the most part, and there is little pupil-to-pupil interaction. Many teachers would like to have their pupils question each other, comment on each other's statements and react to each other with agreement or disagreement, but once again, the necessary skill is often lacking, for the teacher does not know what to say or do to encourage children to listen to and react to one another.

This teacher might have encouraged the youngsters to exchange ideas by dividing them into groups and asking them to discuss the topic. Or she might have said "Let's just take a few minutes and each turn to our neighbor and talk about why people move about."

In the large group discussion, the teacher might encourage pupils to talk to each other by saying such things as, "You know, Bill, your reasons and Barbara's reasons seem to be similar. Will you two take a minute to discuss that while we listen?" Or she might use the ground rule that each pupil statement must be commented upon in some way by another pupil before any other kind of verbal behavior can take place.

SKILL SESSION   Go over the talk in this situation and find places where the teacher might have encouraged pupils to talk to each other, question each other, comment upon each other's statements and so forth. What exactly will the teacher say?

Situation 9

Mrs. Granada said to her seventh graders, "Today we're going to work in groups of four, and we're going to discuss the question, 'If we were scientists who could invent anything at all that we wanted to, what would we invent?' Write down the main ideas from your group and then we'll compare them. All ideas are acceptable. As long as you want something to be invented, it's all right."

When the class had divided up, Rick, Jim, Karl, and Esther formed one group. "I'd invent a money machine so's I could make all the money I want. Then I don't need no other invention," declared Karl.

"That'd be good—but it don't do everything," commented Esther.

"Oh yeah—name me something it don't do."

"Well, money don't cure all the diseases. Like if you get cancer or something all the money in the world ain't gonna cure it."

"Right. So let's have a disease-curing machine too. You get inside the machine and you're cured," suggested Rick.

"Yeah—that'd be great. And how about a disappearing machine —kind of a ray gun. Like you could make schools disappear," was Karl's next suggestion.

"Boy! Wait till Mrs. Granada hears that one!" said Jim.

"Well, she don't need to disappear—she's okay. We could have a machine that'd just make certain people disappear—not the whole school," Karl amended his idea. "Boy, we could make Mr. Green disappear. . . ."

"And Mrs. Cain!" said Barbara.

"Yeah! And how about old Reilly. And Fatso," added Jim.

"Okay, okay. Mrs. Granada wants real ideas. Let's get going. How about a machine that'd make you learn whatever you want to," said Rick.

"Any idea is all right. Mrs. Granada said so. But a homework machine would be good. I could use one right now. I didn't do the math," said Karl.

"Not just a homework machine. A machine that'd make you *know* the stuff. Then doin' the homework'd be easy. We'd already know the answers," Rick said.

"Okay, that'd be a good one for our list," agreed Esther. "And I'd like some kind of machine, or maybe some medicine, that'd make you nice. You know—everybody would like you."

"Who do you want to like you? Larry, I betcha!" grinned Karl.

"Well, everybody would take the medicine and then everybody'd like everybody else," blushed Esther.

"Well, I'd never like Mr. Green," insisted Karl.

"With this invention you would," replied Rick.

"Then I don't want that invention," said Karl.

"The whole group don't have to agree. Put it down—it's a good idea," said Rick.

"All right, boys and girls," Mrs. Granada interrupted. "Let's start getting our suggestions onto the board, and then we'll discuss them. Who wants to be first?"

"We have some good ones," offered Karl. . . ."

ANALYSIS   Use the VICS teacher talk categories to analyze the pupil-to-pupil interaction in this situation.

What effect do you think the small group discussion will have on the total group discussion which follows?

SKILL SESSION   When small groups come together for a total group discussion, it is important for the teacher to be able to accept and summarize pupil talk, and help the pupils classify the ideas which emerge.

Divide into small groups and discuss the question in this situation. "What would we invent if we could invent anything we wished?" Then reconvene, and the person playing the part of the teacher should try to accept, summarize, and help pupils classify their contributions in the large group.

Situation 10A

"Let's all try to participate in this discussion of civil rights," said Mr. Haskell to his ninth grade class. "Say whatever you think and feel, and the rest of us will listen. We'll all have a turn."

"Well, I think one group is getting everything handed to them on a silver platter," began Bob. "My father said they're going to take everybody else's jobs away from them and ruin the neighborhoods and everything like that."

"Do you think that's really true?" asked Mr. Haskell. "From what I have read, I wouldn't say that is the case at all. The American way is to give everybody a fair and equal chance. Now you wouldn't like it if you couldn't go into certain restaurants or to certain schools, would you?"

"I wouldn't care. I'd only go where people wanted me," Nancy said.

"If you think about it for awhile, I think you may change your mind. After all," Mr. Haskell reminded the class, "let's remember that this country is a democracy."

"That's right, and I don't think it's fair. Everybody should have an equal chance," agreed Henrietta.

"Very good, Henrietta," said Mr. Haskell. "That's the kind of attitude I like to see. Who else would like to say something?"

"Well, when I was little I used to play with some kids from the Front Street School and we always had fun. They were okay," responded John.

"Fine, you see, if you just have a chance to know people, you will like them. Anyone else?" asked Mr. Haskell.

"Well, maybe they *are* getting extra money for their schools and things the way Bob said, but they really need it, because they don't have as many things as we do. They don't have such good jobs," said Henrietta.

"Right," commented Mr. Haskell.

"I think they should have extra things to make up for the past," added John.

"That's a good point, John," said Mr. Haskell. "I know that some people say that if you work hard enough you'll get what you want, but that isn't always true. Anyone else? Don't hesitate to express your ideas. Everyone's ideas are just as good as everyone else's, you know. I don't like to see the same people doing all the talking. . . ."

ANALYSIS   Toward the beginning of this situation Mr. Haskell says, "Say whatever you think and feel, and the rest of us will listen." At the end, he says, "I don't like to see the same people doing all the talking. . . ." Use the VICS categories to analyze the situation and see if you can determine why this teacher does not have the wide pupil participation he says he wants.

SKILL SESSION   Divide into groups of two and take turns accepting statements from each other with which you do not agree.

Situation 10B

Mr. Thatcher began a discussion with his ninth graders by saying, "Say whatever you think or feel in this discussion of civil rights, and the rest of us will listen. We'll all have a turn."

"Well, I think one group is getting everything handed to them on a silver platter," began Pat. "My father said they're going to take jobs away from other people, and ruin the neighborhoods and everything like that."

"That's right—they'll move into our neighborhoods and spoil them," said Kate.

"How would they spoil them?" asked Mr. Thatcher.

"Well, they don't take care of their property," answered Pat.

"How about Mayfair Heights?" asked Mr. Thatcher. "Is that well cared for?"

"Okay, but how about Dover Street," replied Diane.

"Well, what about Third Street? They don't live there, and that's one of the worst parts of town," said Joe.

"What do you think accounts for whether neighborhoods are well kept or poorly kept?" asked Mr. Thatcher.

"If people are rich their yards are nice, and if they're poor they're not," said Frank.

"Well, we're not rich and our yard is nice," said Leona.

"Perhaps we could say that very often the neighborhoods of poor people are not as well kept as the neighborhoods of people who are a little better off—no matter who the people are," suggested Mr. Thatcher.

"Yeah, but everybody knows those people have *more* rotten-looking neighborhoods," said Diane.

"Because they have more poor," responded Claire.

"Well, why do they have more poor? Nobody tells them to be poor," said Michael.

"It's harder for them to get jobs," Sharon joined in.

"That's just because they're lazy," replied Michael.

"That's not the only reason," countered Ellen. "My father said that you don't feel like working hard at school and so on if all you can be is a janitor or something when you finish."

"Well, they don't have to be janitors. They can be anything they want," said Ben.

"But most of them are janitors and dishwashers and maids because those are the only jobs they can get," Ellen disagreed. "What if you were the head man in the hospital, let's say. That's what my father was talking about. Well, when it came to doctors and nurses you wouldn't hire them, but for maids and cooks you would."

"Yeah, because that's all they know how to do," said Laura.

"How do you know?" asked Bobby.

"Because that *is* what they do," replied Kate.

"Some of you seem to be saying that certain people have certain jobs because they won't be hired for better jobs, and others are saying that people have certain jobs because that's all they are capable of doing. What about that?" asked Mr. Thatcher.

"Well, we know they can do other things because some of them are doctors and lawyers and teachers and judges and things like that," Alan joined in.

"That proves my point," said Ben. "They can get better jobs if they want."

"But they're too lazy, most of them," agreed Michael.

"What does it take to become a judge or a lawyer?" asked Mr. Thatcher.

"Brains," said Ben.

"Money for college," said Ellen.

"College *and* brains," said Michael.

"Would you want of them to be *your* teacher or *your* doctor, Ellen?" asked Pat.

"Let's think about that question, because it comes up often," suggested Mr. Thatcher. "Why wouldn't some of us want them for our teachers or our doctors? . . ."

ANALYSIS   Contrast the verbal behavior of the teachers in situations 10A and 10B. What accounts for the difference in pupil response in these two classrooms when the same topic is being discussed.

SKILL SESSION   The statement, "People shouldn't go where they aren't wanted," may be responded to with acceptance by saying, "You believe that people should not move into places where they are not welcome," or "That is John's opinion on this subject," or "All right. Would anyone like to comment on that." There are other possible acceptances as well.

Accept the following statements in several ways:

1. Everybody knows those people have *more* rotten-looking neighborhoods.
2. Those people could get better jobs if they wanted to.
3. I don't think schools will really do you any good.
4. Girls are smarter than boys.
5. Voting is a waste of time.

CHAPTER 7
Disciplining

Since so many student teachers and teachers state that discipline is one of their major problems, it might seem that this should be the longest rather than the shortest of the teaching activity chapters. However, if teachers have success with the other teaching activities, they probably will not have many problems with discipline. Discipline problems usually arise because the other teaching activities are not being carried on successfully.

As in each of the groups of situations, this chapter presents some teachers who have more difficulty with the area of disciplining than do others. And, as always, the teacher-pupil talk will be examined to account for differences. In addition to the usual presentation of situations, there is a group of brief verbal exchanges at the end of the chapter which presents teachers dealing differently with exactly the same pupil talk. Some of the teachers are accepting, others are rejecting.

Rejection is a form of punishment, though the rejection may range from mild to severe, and what may be mild for one youngster might be severe for another. Reward is a form of acceptance, but not synonymous with it. For example, if a teacher *accepts* a child's feeling of anger, this does not mean that he is rewarding that behavior.

For most teachers, learning to be positive when dealing with problems of discipline, rather than negative, is very much an acquired skill. The past experience of most people, both in and out of school, seems to have been that "wrong" behavior was punished, while "right" behavior may have been ignored. It is difficult to avoid the "don'ts" and concentrate on the "do's." Even though our prisons are filled with people being treated with strongly negative disciplinary measures, the behavior of the inmates seldom seems to change when they are released—as shown by the high rates of recidivism. Yet it is hard for the public to give up the idea that punishment—that is, strong negative disciplinary measures—will change people.

Of course teachers must have control (in the sense of responsiveness) in their classrooms in order to carry on their teaching activities. However, unless the pupils respond because of their interest and because the teacher is a human being to whom they want to respond, much pupil potential will be lost, and many negative learnings may accompany whatever subject matter learnings do occur.

Situation 1

When Miss Wallace took her kindergarten children to the gymnasium for the first time the boys and girls arrived in a quiet and organized fashion, but when she said, "We're going to play a game now in this room," the children reacted by running about the gym and shouting and laughing, before Miss Wallace could explain the game she had in mind.

"Children! Stop this instant! Do you hear me? I said that's enough! Billy—Johnny—Brenda, I said to stop," Miss Wallace called frantically.

She clutched a few children and told them to sit down on the sidelines. But the others kept running and made so much noise that she couldn't make herself heard above the din. She continued to grab a few children here and there, but she noticed that some of those whom she had seated earlier had rejoined the running crowd.

"I said to stop and I meant it! Now listen, children, sit down and be quiet!" she kept shouting ineffectually.

Finally after four or five minutes of grabbing and scolding, Miss Wallace managed to seat everyone at the sides of the huge gym. The children had tired of running, and this made them easier to subdue.

"This is absolutely the last time we will ever come here. I am ashamed of you and the way you behaved," scolded Miss Wallace. "I never saw anything like it! Now, when I call your name, you will come up quietly, you will get into a straight line, and you will walk back through the halls without making a sound. And we will *never, ever* come into this room again. It's too bad, because I had some nice games planned for you. However, since you can't behave you'll have to miss all the fun. Now, remember what I said. Not a peep from anyone. These children may get into line. . . ."

ANALYSIS   Some of the teacher statements in this situation, although they superficially appear to be directions, are actually rejections. "Stop this instant!" is categorized as rejection of behavior because the teacher is saying, "Stop that undesirable behavior and do something more desirable," and whenever a teacher communicates that, then the talk is rejection rather than direction. "Do you hear me?" is also a rejection— the teacher is rejecting their nonlistening behavior. Can you find the one sentence in this case which is a true direction?

What kinds of statements are these: "And we will *never, ever* come into this room again. It's too bad because I had some nice games planned for you. However, since you can't behave you'll have to miss all the fun."

Why do you think this teacher became so upset when the children began to run around the gym?

SKILL SESSION   Role play a discussion with this class after they have returned from the gymnasium, in which the teacher asks questions which are designed to bring out the feelings of the children about the experience they have just had. The pupils might have feelings of guilt, anger, disappointment, frustration, confusion. The teacher should accept all feelings.

Situation 2

Miss Moore's first grade class was having reading time, and she was working with one reading group in a corner of the room, while the rest of the children worked at their seats.

"Clifford, you and Ernie will have to be quiet. We can't hear ourselves talk up here. And I don't want to have to speak to you again." Miss Moore turned back to her reading group and continued to work with them, but a few minutes later she called to some of the children in their seats, "Sue, stop dreaming and get to work. And you too, Larry. Stop fooling around."

Miss Moore turned again to the reading group, but soon she spoke once more to some children doing seat work. "Tommy, get quiet and get to work. No talking out there! And Clifford, this is the second time I've spoken to you. Get busy!"

Again it was back to the reading group, but only for a few minutes. Then Miss Moore stood up and announced, "I've had enough. You are too noisy, and I'm tired of it. How do you think we're supposed to hear when you keep talking? I want every single one of you to put your heads down on your desks and I don't want to hear another sound. Does everyone understand? Heads down for the rest of the reading period!" And with a sigh she turned back to her reading group.

ANALYSIS   In this situation, as in situation 1, many of the teacher statements which may appear on the surface to be directions are in reality rejections. For instance, "Sue, stop dreaming and get to work," is a teacher statement which rejects a pupil behavior. It is not a direction. Directions are more neutral, more non-emotional.

This teacher uses few categories to try to control her pupils' behavior. When teachers try to discipline their classes they apparently feel that certain verbal behavior is most appropriate, and this behavior is rejection. Why is it that verbal behavior which is rejecting often does not accomplish what teachers expect it to?

SKILL SESSION   Go through this situation carefully and determine what other category or categories this teacher might have used with more effectiveness. For instance, she might have said, "Clifford, can I help you and Ernie in any way?" rather than, "Clifford, you and Ernie will have to be quiet."

Situation 3

Miss Jones, a student teacher, was discussing sound, and the way in which it traveled, with her third grade class. She began by passing out some rulers, and rubber bands and a variety of other materials.

There was a good deal of noise and confusion, and fussing over who would have what. A typical exchange between the children was, "She gave *me* that ruler—not you!" "She did not—and she said we have to share, anyway." The arguments were accompanied by much grabbing and retaking of materials.

Finally, Miss Jones said, "You know children, I've worked hard for you but I don't care whether we go on with this or not. I already know about sound, and if you're not interested in learning, I certainly don't care. I'm just going to stand here and wait until you're ready, even if it takes all morning." And she folded her arms and waited.

The children, unimpressed by her statement, continued with their bickering and noise. A few duelists went into action using their rulers, and they were soon joined by some rubber-band snappers. Miss Jones continued to stand in front of the room determined to look unconcerned in the midst of bedlam.

ANALYSIS   This situation is similar to the first two situations in this section in that there is a good deal of confusion, which the teacher attempts to handle with the category of rejection. When a teacher speaks of how hard he has tried and how disappointed he is because the children are so ungrateful, that is categorized as rejection. Teachers often take pupils' misbehavior as a personal insult, even though they may not be consciously aware that they feel rejected by the pupils.
What might be the consequences of this teacher's action?

SKILL SESSION   Change these highly personal statements into more objective statements:

1. If you don't stop talking you'll make Mrs. Smith very unhappy.
2. I've worked hard on this trip and now you're spoiling it.
3. You never listen to me.
4. I'm very disappointed in your behavior.
5. I don't know why I keep trying to plan interesting things for you, when you don't appreciate them.

Situation 4A

"Open your spelling books to page 24," said Miss Andrews to her fourth grade class. "Quickly—what's the problem there? As usual, you have the wrong book, George. Don't you ever listen? What's so funny, Ann? We don't have private jokes in this class. You don't even have the right page, Roger. Perhaps someday you'll do what the rest of us are doing!"

"Paul, spell the first word."

The word was "walking," but Paul grinned and said, "Wall king, w-a-l-k-i-n-g, wall king."

The class laughed at this purposeful mispronunciation.

"You know very well how that word is pronounced, Paul, but as usual you have to try to be funny. And the rest of you shouldn't encourage him by laughing. Jack, give us the next word."

"Tall king, t-a-l-k-i-n-g, tall king," responded Jack.

More laughter greeted this recitation.

"All right, since you people want to act so smart, you can just close your books and I'll give you something to really laugh about. We're going to have a spelling test right now. Maybe you won't think that's so funny!"

ANALYSIS A common but usually ineffectual verbal pattern of many teachers who have discipline problems is that of giving direction, followed by rejection of inappropriate pupil behavior, followed by further direction, followed by still more rejection of pupil behavior. Even though this pattern usually prevents teachers from reaching their intended goals, they seem to have difficulty extricating themselves in order to try new approaches. The pattern is, of course, not limited to teachers, but is common throughout our culture when people try to deal with other people's behavior which they want to change.

Symonds gives some examples of what he calls negative instruction, such as, "No! No! That is not the way I told you to do it," and "When is this class going to get over this terrible habit?" He considers these kinds of statements to be inefficient unless followed by further teacher talk which explains what is correct or expected. "Instead of clearly telling a child what is wrong—and more important, what is right—these teachers make the issue a personal one by an attack on the child. Each of these remarks should serve to hurt the child, to arouse him emotionally, to stimulate tendencies toward counterattack or self-defence, and hence to interfere with the learning process." [1]

SKILL SESSION Instead of saying, "You are on the wrong page, as usual," a teacher will probably accomplish more if he says, "The correct page is 29. It's the page right opposite this map."

Modify the following statements so that they help pupils to achieve the desired behavior.

[1] Percival M. Symonds, *What Education Has to Learn from Psychology* (New York: Bureau of Publications, Teachers College, Columbia University, 1958), p. 35.

1. Why is it that you never pay attention?
2. Is that the way to open a book?
3. You folded your paper the wrong way.
4. We don't open the door that way.
5. You made all your lines wrong.
6. That's not the way I said to do it.
7. Don't walk like that.

Situation 4B

"Open your spelling books to page 24," said Miss Rafferty to her fourth grade class. As she moved about among the children she held her book open to the proper page and helped certain children put their other things away and take the proper book from their desks. "You'll have to put that away now, Bill. Can you finish it before class this afternoon? Jean, your speller is at the bottom of that pile. Perhaps you can clean your desk out today so that you can see what you have in there. Tom, will you share your book with Brad today, and you can help each other keep the place."

"Fine, I think we all have the page now. It's this one with the picture of the boy and girl at the top. Let's start with this row today. Jud, will you be first?"

"Wall king, w-a-l-k-i-n-g, wall king," said Jud with a grin.

The class laughed at this purposeful mispronunciation, and Miss Rafferty joined in. "We know it's really pronounced 'wah'king,' " she said, "but if we pronounced it the way it looks we certainly would say 'wall king.' That's why English spelling presents so many problems and why the words have to be studied. Do you remember what we said about many of the words which are spelled differently from the way they sound?"

"Once, probably a long time ago, the words were pronounced that way," answered one of the pupils.

"So words which seem odd to us now were probably once pronounced according to the way they are now spelled, but speech changes faster than spelling, and the result is that we are stuck with a hard subject. Well, we've had our fun, and now let's pronounce the rest of the words according to today's styles. Ed, will you be next."

"Talking, t-a-l-k-i-n-g, talking."

"Now—who would like to make up a two-sentence rhyme using those two words? . . ."

ANALYSIS Contrast the verbal interaction in this situation with that in situation 4A. What categories used by the teacher in situation 4B seem to make the difference in the way the pupils respond to direction?

What seem to be the assumptions of these two teachers about helping pupils follow direction? What are the consequences of these assumptions?

SKILL SESSION When pupils give answers or make statements which are silly, or which teachers regard as impertinent, there are several ways to respond. It is probable that most teachers respond with rejection, but the teacher in this case laughs with the class when Jud purposely mispronounces a word—which is equivalent to accepting the feeling of the class—and then she accepts that part of his answer which is sensible.

Extend the following teacher-pupil exchanges by having the teacher respond without rejection:

Teacher	Who knows why we celebrate Washington's birthday?
Pupil	Because we don't have to come to school that day.
Teacher	Why are we going on this trip?
Pupil	Because we paid for the bus.
Teacher	Why should you be quiet in the halls?
Pupil	So Mr. Jones won't holler at us.
Teacher	What's the best way to travel from here to Texas?
Pupil	By Pony Express.
Teacher	Let's open our books to page 10.
Pupil	Let's close them on page 10, instead.

Situation 5

"Some of the members of this class have been doing quite a bit of noisy fooling around lately, and it's becoming annoying," said Miss Hughes to her fifth grade class as the school day drew to a close. "I keep speaking to the same children over and over

again. It seems too bad that the rest of us have to be constantly interrupted and bothered by these few. Maybe some of you have some suggestions for what to do about this problem."

"You could make the kids who talk all the time sit on the floor
in the back of the room."

"Or you could send them to the principal. That's what Mr. Grey
used to do."

"They shouldn't be allowed to come to school if they can't behave."

"You could make them stay in the coat room or out in the hall."

"They could stand by their desks until they could be quiet, and
also their mothers should have to come to school."

"They could have extra pages of work, and extra homework."

"They could stay after school."

"Well, we have a number of suggestions," said Miss Hughes. "But
you know, I've noticed that those kinds of punishments often don't
work—especially with those who make the most noise or pay the least
attention. I remember when I was in school, the same children stayed
after school day after day, but they didn't change. And that was true
if they were sent to the principal or even sent home. Their behavior
didn't seem to improve. Maybe we could come up with some new ideas
—something besides punishment."

"But if you don't punish them they'll do it more."

"It's not fair to get away with things."

"Yeah, but you're right about the same kids getting all the punishments and they're still the same way they were in kindergarten."

"So what'll we do—give the bad kids some prizes?"

"Well, perhaps we could start by finding out why they are noisy
and why they don't pay attention more," suggested Miss Hughes. "But
the bell's about to ring, so let's think about this overnight, and tomorrow morning, first thing, we'll talk more about this. Maybe we'll
really be able to do some important problem solving. Those who have
been reprimanded so often lately can think about why this has happened to you, and we'll all talk the thing over together."

ANALYSIS   Describe the talk in this situation by referring to the categories in the VICS.
            What might be some effects of this open
discussion on the behavior of the children who are causing problems
in the classroom? What seem to be some of this teacher's assumptions
about methods of disciplining?

Why is it that many children who are re-
proved and punished most seem not to improve, and even may display increased misbehavior?

SKILL SESSION   Role play the next session of this class, with the
first statement of the teacher being, "Yesterday we said that we would
go on with our discussion about why some of you have been noisier
than you should be. I suggested that the people who have been reprimanded so often lately might think about why this has happened.
And we'll see what suggestions we have for trying to change behavior.
Who would like to begin?"

Situation 6

"What's wrong, Mildred?" asked Mr. Mac-
Donald as one of the girls in his sixth grade class came into the room
crying during the lunch hour.

"They won't leave me alone."

"Who won't leave you alone?"

"The other kids."

"You mean the whole class?"

"They called me names, and they don't want me to be on their
side."

"Didn't anyone choose you for a team?"

"Well, I'm always the last one—and nobody wants me to play.
They choose me because they know they have to. They said I'm too
fat, and I can't run, and they called me a hippo," sobbed Mildred.

"Well, don't you worry, Mildred," said Mr. MacDonald. "When
the children come in after lunch *I'll* take care of *them*. A few days of
sitting inside during lunch hour will teach them a thing or two about
how to treat people."

ANALYSIS   This teacher seems to assume that the pupils in his class
will treat Mildred with more consideration if he takes some privileges
away from them. What do you think of this as a method for helping
children treat their classmates with respect? What else could this
teacher say to Mildred, and later to the class?

SKILL SESSION   Reject the behavior, but accept the feelings in the
following statements:

1. I don't like Joe, because he's so fat.
2. Why does he have to play? He can't even hit straight.
3. Well, with her on our side, we're sure to lose.
4. Why does he have to be in our group? He's too silly.
5. Our report won't be any good if we have to have Gail on our committee.
6. I don't like him. He can't borrow any of my crayons.
7. I won't be in that old play. The other kids will laugh at me.
8. I'll be your friend if you show me your paper.

Situation 7

"Put away your geography books and papers," Mr. Gregory said to his seventh grade class, "and turn to. . . ."

"I didn't have time to finish," "Me neither," "Wait a minute—it's not fair," "We never have enough time," were some comments heard from the children.

"What is all this? I asked you to put your things away—now do as I say," Mr. Gregory demanded. "You should have had enough time to finish. If you didn't you can take your things home with you and finish there."

"Aw gee whiz—I've got too much stuff to take home *now*," muttered one child.

"No more complaining! Get your desks cleared immediately. We have to get ready for gym. Let's hurry or we'll be late again. Row one—get your sneaks."

There was a considerable amount of scuffling and pushing as row one went for their gym shoes.

"Row one! Sit down!" bellowed Mr. Gregory. "What's all this noise? This class can't seem to do anything without getting into trouble. Even the simplest thing can't be done by you people without all kinds of fuss. No wonder we're always late. Now, I've said this to you several times in the past few days, but this time I mean it. If you can't settle down immediately and do as you're told, you will have *no* class picnic next week. And that's final!"

ANALYSIS   Analyze the talk in this situation by referring to the VICS categories. What pattern is present which we have mentioned before as common yet ineffectual teacher behavior for changing pupils' behavior? The pattern which you find in this case is one which may well cause misbehavior rather than cure it.

Teachers often threaten children with loss of various privileges if they do not behave as the teacher wishes, and less often, they punish children by denying them privileges. What do you think of the long-run effect of these methods? Are they ever appropriate?

SKILL SESSION

1. Follow each direction in this situation with positive feedback of some kind.
2. Modify each direction in this situation so that it is stated in question form.
3. Modify each rejecting teacher statement to remove the rejection.

Situation 8A

Mr. Moffet's ninth graders had been reported for not passing through the halls quietly enough, and for talking excessively when they arrived in science class.

"Well, boys and girls, this is the second time this has happened. You know the rules. Tomorrow afternoon everybody stays after school —no exceptions. So make whatever arrangements are necessary. Bus people, be sure to tell your parents that you'll be taking the late bus home."

After school the next day, Mr. Moffet's class gathered in its homeroom.

"All right, now, we have an hour to spend here," said Mr. Moffet. "Everyone get out homework and get busy. I have a lot of work to do up here and I don't expect to be disturbed. I know that everyone of you has something he can do—so get busy. And maybe you'll be more careful from now on about the way you walk in the halls and the way you behave when you get into other teachers' rooms."

ANALYSIS What categories does this teacher use according to the VICS?

A related analysis and skill session will be found after situation 8B.

Situation 8B

Mr. Lomanski's ninth graders had been reported for not passing through the halls quietly enough, and for talking excessively when they arrived in science class.

"Boys and girls, this is the second time this has happened. And that means an afternoon after school, as you know. Tomorrow will be the day, so everyone had better make the proper arrangements—with no exceptions. And don't forget to tell your parents that you'll be home on the late bus—those of you who ride the bus."

After school the next day Mr. Lomanski's class gathered in its homeroom.

"Well, here we are, staying after school," Mr. Lomanski said to his class as they settled in their seats. "Would someone like to review the reasons?"

"Noisy in the halls." "Noisy in Mr. Vesey's room."

"And it's not fair to keep everybody in. I didn't even talk."

"You may be right," said Mr. Lomanski, "but it's a school rule for second offenses, as you know. Now—what can we do to avoid this happening in the future?"

"Get certain kids to shut up!"

"Yeah—they think they're so smart."

"And how are we going to accomplish this goal?" inquired Mr. Lomanski.

"Put gags in their mouths."

"Let's talk seriously. Does anyone have any suggestions?" asked Mr. Lomanski again. "How about the ones who were doing the talking?"

"I don't see why we can't talk in the halls. What is this? A reform school? We weren't yelling—we were just talking to each other."

"And that Mr. Vesey is a pain! He's so strict you can't even *move* in his class."

"Well, I can't help you about Mr. Vesey. Except to remind you that different teachers expect different behavior, and you just have to adapt your habits accordingly. As for talking in the halls—any suggestions about that?"

"Why don't we bring it up before the student council—or the principal, or something?"

"Yeah—the student council. I'm the representative this month, and I could suggest something."

"What would you suggest?" Mr. Lomanski asked.

"Well, I could say that there isn't really any reason for absolute quiet in the halls when we change classes. No classes are in session, so it's silly. And we're old enough to be allowed to talk quietly."

"Does that meet with your approval?" The class nodded its agreement. "But in the meantime," Mr. Lomanski reminded the class, "the rule is 'no talking' and we have to stick to it. Do you think you can?"

"Yeah," "I guess so," came the responses.

"Okay—now take out whatever work you have to do and get started. You can work together if you do so quietly—but stick to *work*. I'll be up at my desk if anybody wants any help."

ANALYSIS Analyze this situation thoroughly by referring to the VICS categories. Compare Mr. Lomanski's verbal behavior with that of Mr. Moffet, the teacher in Situation 8A. What seem to be some of the underlying assumptions of the two teachers about the value and use of the disciplinary measure which their classes have received?

SKILL SESSION In order to consciously improve your ability to select the verbal behavior you wish to use, take each teacher category in Situation 8B and modify it so that it will fall into some other VICS category.

SOME BRIEF CONTRASTING EXAMPLES

The following short situations are presented as contrasting examples of how different teachers might handle the same situation. Discuss each pair of cases in terms of the VICS categories, and discuss also the teachers' assumptions about discipline and the consequences of the differing verbal behavior.

Situation A

"I don't like you," Steve announced to the teacher as she told him to leave the block corner.

"How dare you speak to me like that! We don't talk to teachers that way in this school! Is that the kind of manners you have? Now just get to your seat and stay there until I tell you to get up again."

Situation AA

"I don't like you," Steve announced to the teacher as she told him to leave the block corner.

"You're angry with me now, I know. But you can't knock over the buildings that other children have worked hard to build. To-morrow you can have another try at building, but for now you'll have to try something else. How about coming over here with me to the easel—I have to mix some new paint, and you can help."

Situation B

"Read the next sentence, Mark," said the teacher to a child who wasn't looking at his book. "You don't even know where we are. Go back to your seat and maybe tomorrow you'll pay attention! Lois, you read the next sentence."

"There was a small green ball," Lois read.

"No, no. Look at that word again. You're not looking. What's that last word?"

"Ball?"

"You just can't seem to get it right, Lois. If you'd pay attention instead of dreaming, you'd know that word. Who can tell Lois what that word is?"

"Bell," said another child.

"Good. You've been paying attention. You may continue reading."

Situation BB

"Read the next sentence, Lois," said the teacher. "We're right here at this word."

"There was a small green ball," Lois read.

"That last word does look very much like ball, but it has an important difference. I'll write the word 'ball' and the other word here on the board. What is different about them, Lois?"

"One has an 'e' and one has an 'a.' "

"Yes, 'ball' has an 'a' and this word has 'e.' " What sound does 'e' usually make? We hear it in 'tell' and 'sell.' "

"Oh—the word is 'bell.' "

"All right. You can continue reading, Lois."

Situation C

"Edith is a sneaky rat, and we won't play with her," said Gail.

"What kind of language is that?" asked the teacher. "And since when do you decide with whom you will and will not play in this school? You will play with the people I tell you to play with, or you won't play at all. Now, just for those words, Edith can join the game, but you can leave it, young lady. Stand by the door until it's time to go inside."

Situation CC

"Edith is a sneaky rat, and we won't play with her," said Gail.

"Well, you seem to have some strong feelings about Edith. What's the problem?" asked the teacher.

"She told Barbara that I said Barbara wasn't my friend."

"What about that, Edith?"

"I didn't. I just said *maybe* she wasn't Barbara's friend."

"Edith, do you want to be the friend of these girls?" asked the teacher.

"Yes, and I want to play," Edith fought back some tears.

"Well, Gail, how about it? We all say things, sometimes, that perhaps shouldn't be said. Edith would like to play along with you."

"Well, okay, but she better not tell any more stories about me."

"I think Edith can try that. All right? Why don't I turn the jump rope for awhile?"

Situation D

"Go to your seat, Victor," said the teacher.

"No, I don't want to."

"What do you mean, you don't want to! Don't ever say no to me!

Now you just get into the hall and stay there until I'm ready to have you back in this room again."

Victor walked out of the room as slowly as discretion allowed, his turned face expressing the words he didn't dare speak.

Situation DD

"Go to your seat, Victor," said the teacher.

"No, I don't want to."

"Why not?"

"I'm tired of sitting down—and I'm tired of reading."

"Well, perhaps you have been sitting too long today. Why don't you spend some time organizing the library—it's kind of a mess again. The last time you fixed it up so well. Then when you're ready to start your work again, you can sit down."

Situation E

"What's the answer to the next problem, Kay?" asked the teacher.

"I didn't get that far in my homework last night."

"All right, double the homework assignment for you tonight. Instead of the first ten examples, you do all twenty. Robert, you tell us the answer."

"I didn't do it either."

"Well you've forgotten your homework once too often, young man. You can take yourself down to the principal's office right now. Maybe that will help you do your assignments. Here's a note—now take your books and leave immediately."

Situation EE

"What's the answer to the next problem, Kay?" asked the teacher.

"I didn't get that far in my homework last night."

"I've asked that people who have not done their assignments let me know at the beginning of the period, Kay. See me after class, please. Robert, you tell us the answer."

"I didn't do it either."

"We'd better stop right now and have a talk about our homework assignments. Some people always do their work; some people miss once in awhile, which I can understand, though I would appreciate your speaking to me before we begin instead of sitting there hoping that you won't be called on. And some people fail to do assignments far more than they should. Now, I know that you must have reasons for this, and we had better discuss these reasons. I'm going to ask some of you to move into these seats so that we can talk, while the rest of the class goes on with the work on the next page. Let's see . . . these people need to participate in this discussion . . . Robert, Lew, Kay, Evan. . . ."

ANALYSIS Most classroom disciplinary measures involve behavior or feelings. In each of these pairs of short situations one teacher largely rejects the behavior or feelings of pupils, while the other teacher responds in a variety of ways. List the VICS categories which the second teacher in each pair of cases uses in talking with the pupil or pupils involved.

CHAPTER 8

Counseling

Some educators deprecate any teacher responsibility for pupil development in social and emotional areas, saying that teaching should concern itself with cognitive learning. However, there is a great deal of evidence to show that much cognitive learning will be lost if the social and emotional development of pupils is not dealt with in the classroom, and so this book includes counseling as well as disciplining among the teaching activities. Of course teachers are not primarily counselors or therapists, but they must recognize and work with pupil feelings if they are to help pupils fully utilize their intellectual potential.

It is clear, in this age, that the social and emotional development of man has not kept pace with man's intellectual and technological accomplishments. To say that social and emotional learnings are not the province of the schools seems highly unrealistic if one is concerned about cognitive development, and seems tragic if one is concerned about mankind's fate.

Dealing with pupils' feelings in positive and helpful ways requires skill which can be learned. The situations in this section will provide you with an opportunity to examine various ways in which teachers attempt to counsel pupils, and you will be helped to analyze the verbal behavior of others in addition to practicing your own verbal behavior in counseling situations. As in the previous chapter, there are a number of brief situations at the end which present teachers displaying quite different verbal behavior in similar circumstances.

Situation 1

"What happened, Bobby?" asked Miss Ashley as one of the kindergarten children came up to her with tears in his eyes. "Why are you crying?"

"The kids were pushing me. They always pick on me. Nobody likes me," he sobbed.

Miss Ashley, thinking that unfortunately Bobby's assessment of his popularity was pretty accurate, put her arm around him. "I guess you feel as if nobody likes you today. And that the children are picking on you."

"Nobody does like me. Nobody is my friend. The only friend I have on my whole block is a dog," Bobby reflected sadly.

"Sometimes we do feel that no one cares about us. But I'm your friend, Bobby. And I like you. Tell me about the dog on your block. Whose dog is he?"

"He belongs to the people across the street, but he follows me all around and he plays with me. He really likes me."

"He's almost like your own dog, isn't he?" commented Miss Ashley. "It's nice to have a dog for a friend."

"He brings me a ball, and I throw it for him. He likes to chase the ball all day long. He can chase it over and over."

"It sounds to me as if you have a good time together," said Miss Ashley. "Why don't we go over to the library table where Freddy is, and see if we can find a good story. I think there are some new ones there about dogs, and you can help me pick one out for story time. Maybe we can look it over a little now, and perhaps you can tell part of it to the others. We could share the story-telling time."

"Maybe I could even tell about the dog across the street," Bobby suggested as he accompanied Miss Ashley to the library table.

ANALYSIS   In this situation Miss Ashley is faced with the problem of helping a child deal with his feelings of rejection. She accepts his feelings and lets him know that it is all right to have these feelings. What else does she do to help him?

SKILL SESSION   There are several ways of accepting feeling. One might *identify* with the person by saying such things as, "I think I know how you feel," or "I understand why you are crying," or "I can see why you are so delighted," or "That's happened to me and it is upsetting." One might *objectively reflect* what the other person says he feels, or what his feelings seem to be by saying, "You feel rather unhappy about it," or "You feel that it isn't fair," or "You're very happy today," or "You're terribly angry now." One can *provide encouragement* simply by giving evidence of listening with interest, by saying such things as, "Yes," "Um hum," and "I see." Use the three methods of accepting feelings just described with the following statements:

1. I used to like him.
2. I had a good time at the circus.
3. I never have any fun.
4. Who cares if he won. He's not so hot.
5. He used to like me.
6. I'm glad we can all go.
7. He's not very nice.
8. I wish I could go to the circus.
9. I'm glad he isn't going with us.
10. She told me I was nice.

Situation 2

"Boys and girls," said Miss Beam to her first grade class, "I saw part of a show on television the other night that showed a group of children playing tag, and another child came along and asked to play, but the others said no. Well, I had to go out then and I didn't see the rest of the program, so I don't know what happened. And I've been wondering about it. What do you think might have happened?"

"They probably had a fight."

"The other kid went home."

"Maybe he wasn't very nice."

"He told the other kids they were bad."

"Maybe some of you would like to *show* the rest of us what you think happened next. We can play it out as we have at other times. Who wants to try? All right, suppose we have Len be the child who asks to play and Stan, Jean, and Robert be the other children."

Those children came to the front of the room and began,

"Can I play?" asked Len.

"No, we don't want you."

"But I want to play."

"Get out of here—you can't play." And Len was pushed.

"But I want to play."

"Well you can't."

"All right," Miss Beam stopped the action, "these people have shown us their ideas about what might have happened. Are there any other ideas? Let's have Rena be the child who asks to play, and Peter, Wanda, and May be the others."

"Can I play with you?"

"No, we don't want you."

"I'll be your friend if you let me play."

"No. Get your own game."

"Please?"

"Well—okay. But you have to do what we say."

"All right," said Miss Beam. "Have any of the rest of you thought of other ways it might have happened? This will be the last acting out. Charles can be the child who asks to play, and let's have Larry, Grace, and Tina be the others."

"Can I play tag?"

"No, we don't want you."

"Then I won't be your friend."

"Who cares!"

"You're mean."

"Well we don't want you."

"I'm going to tell your mother."

"Now these people have showed us still another version of what might have happened. Let's talk about this for awhile," suggested Miss Beam. "Have you ever been left out of a game, or kept someone else out? And do you have any other ideas about what might have happened on that TV show that I saw?"

"My sister never wants me to play with her. She's mean."

"We don't let this kid on our block play with us, because he's terrible. We don't like him."

"I think that they should have let the other person play with them, because it was only tag. And it's no fun if you can't play."

"Is it ever fun to keep someone out of a game?" asked Miss Beam.

"Sometimes. I don't want to play with my cousin, so I hide on him."

"Yeah—we all run away from a kid on my street, and that's fun."

"So sometimes it's fun to try to keep someone out of a game. How do you think the child who is left out feels? Len and Rena and Charles, how did you feel about being left out?" inquired Miss Beam.

"Well, I wanted to play. It's not nice when they don't want you," said Rena.

"I didn't feel good," said Len, and Charles nodded agreement.

"Does the person who keeps others out always feel good?" was the next question.

"No. Sometimes you don't feel good. You should let the kids play with you."

"My mother made me go and say I was sorry when I wouldn't play with the girl next door."

"If they cry, you might feel sorry."

"So the children who won't let another child play might feel glad about what they did, or they might feel sorry. What about the child who is left out? Will he be happy sometimes?"

"No, he'd never feel glad."

"He wouldn't be happy."

"He'd probably always cry or something like that."

"How can he like it if the other kids won't play with him?"

"Then you seem to be saying that the child who is left out is always made unhappy, and that the children who keep him out might feel glad about what they've done, or they might feel sorry about what they've done. When we are the ones left out we think the other kids are mean, but sometimes we like the feeling of keeping others out. And sometimes we feel sorry when we keep others out. Well, your ideas about what might have happened were very interesting. In a day or two I think we'll do more acting out of this kind of problem."

ANALYSIS Role playing is often an effective counseling technique. It is especially appropriate for helping children understand how people feel in certain situations.

Much of the pattern in this situation is pupil-to-pupil interaction followed by teacher acceptance. Note that the teacher uses no praising or rejecting statements after the role playing. Look carefully at her statements. She avoids any statements which would lead children to believe that there was a good or bad, or right or wrong method for performing in the role playing sessions. She wants the children to spontaneously play out their ideas, not try to guess what the teacher is looking for.

Notice the teacher statement, "So sometimes it's fun to try to keep someone out of a game, "a response which accepts the feelings expressed by some of the children. The teacher then helps the class understand how the rejected child might feel by asking, "How do you think the child who is left out feels? Len and Rena and Charles, how did you feel about being left out?" But there is no moralizing about any of the children's feelings or statements.

The final paragraph is a summary of what has happened, stated in accepting terms, without praise or rejection, other than the rather neutral, "Well, your ideas about what might have happened were very interesting."

SKILL SESSION   Think of some situations from your own experience which involve children having problems with other children. Develop these into story form and then construct some appropriate questions or statements designed to help children express the feelings of the characters, and their own feelings. For instance, you might say, "How do you feel about that?" or "Does anyone know how Ronnie felt then?" or "How do you feel when. . . ."

Situation 3

Mrs. Nichols was talking with three of her second grade boys whom she had asked to come to school fifteen minutes early each morning. She had decided upon these meetings because the boys were so consistently disruptive in class; talking out, finding it difficult to sit still, bothering the people near them and seldom finishing their work. This meeting was their third.

"You know, boys, I think I see a difference already," Mrs. Nichols began. "Neal, you and Kerry finished all the work I assigned you yesterday, and Russ finished all but two examples. Now, when we come to today's assignment of seat work, shall we use the same system—you boys will have a shorter assignment, but you'll really finish?"

"Yes," came from Russ and Kerry.

"I bet I could do everything by now," declared Neal.

"Well, let's wait another day or two, Neal. Let's go slowly on this experiment. However, you certainly are doing your work. Now, what about milk time? It seems that Russ still had some trouble yesterday."

"Yeah, he still was getting out of his seat all the time, and I saw him shoot his straw paper to the other side of the room."

"Well, there's nothing to do," Russ defended himself, "and I finish my milk before the rest."

"Can you think of something that you might do if you finish first?" asked Mrs. Nichols. "What do the other children do?"

"We're supposed to talk quietly to the people around us till everybody's through. But it's too long to wait."

"Perhaps we can try something else for you, Russ," Mrs. Nichols suggested. "What else could you do at that time?"

"I could collect all the milk cartons," said Russ.

"That's not fair. Everybody's supposed to have a turn with that job," objected Kerry.

"Yes, Russ, everyone likes that job, so it wouldn't be fair if you had it every day," agreed Mrs. Nichols.

"Maybe he could clean something in the room—like the library corner or something like that," said Neal.

"How about that, Russ?" asked Mrs. Nichols. "There's always something to be done around the room."

"Okay, that's good. I could clean the coat room too. The kids are always knocking down the coats."

"Have you boys thought any more about why it's so difficult for you to listen sometimes—why you have a hard time sitting still?" Mrs. Nichols inquired.

"I told my mother what we talked about here, and she said I never sat still from the day I was born. I don't know why. But it's more fun to do other things—who wants to sit?" came from Russ.

"Well, sometimes I sit still, like when I watch television," said Neal.

"And I've noticed," commented Mrs. Nichols, "that you all sit quietly during story time. Why is that?"

"I like it."

"I want to hear the story."

"Yeah—a story is good."

"What would happen if none of the children in our room sat still or listened except when they felt like it?" was Mrs. Nichols' next question.

"It would be a mess!"

"It'd be like recess time."

"Well, why would that matter?" probed Mrs. Nichols.

"Because you have to learn to read and write and those things."

"Do you think it's harder for some people to sit still than others?" continued Mrs. Nichols.

"Sure—you can see that. Some kids don't care if they sit all day."

"Do you think you might be able to learn to sit for longer periods of time if you really try?" Mrs. Nichols asked the boys.

"I think *I* could."

"Maybe."

"Well, let's give it a try. I won't expect you to change immediately, but I am going to look for some improvement. In the meantime, let's continue our meetings for a while."

"Yeah, let's."

"I like this time."

"Me too."

ANALYSIS Describe the talk in this situation by referring to the VICS categories. Notice that many of the teacher's responses would not be categorized as either acceptance or rejection.

What does this kind of conference do that could not be accomplished during the regular school day?

Discuss the idea of giving pupils shorter assignments because they do not finish their work.

SKILL SESSION Divide into groups of four and role play a conference between a teacher and two pupils who cannot get along with each other and who are generally disruptive in class. The fourth person will be the observer. The latest misbehavior of the two pupils has involved a quarrel over whose turn it was to collect the papers in their row, and the result was some ripped test papers. The teacher will attempt to use verbal behavior which contains no rejection of feeling, but may contain rejection of behavior, and he will try to help the pupils talk about their feelings.

Situation 4

A new pupil was going to be enrolled in Mr. Clancy's third grade class in a few days, and he decided to prepare for the girl's arrival by using some role playing and an unfinished story. The class had had good results with these activities before in preparing for coming events, and in dealing with already existing problems.

Mr. Clancy began the activity by saying, "I have a story here without an ending, and I'd like to read it to you. Remember the last one we had—about the boy who couldn't read well? This one is about a girl named Paula. Paula lived with her family in a nice city, and she went to a school nearby, where she had quite a few friends. She liked going to school and meeting her friends and playing with them after school. Well, one day her father came home from work and said, 'We're going to move. I've been promoted and I have a better job in a different city, so as soon as we find a house in the new city we're going there.' Well, Paula and her brothers and sisters were not happy about this. They didn't want to leave their friends and their old house and neighborhood. Their father noticed the sad looks on their faces, and he said, 'What's the matter? Why those long faces? Moving is fun. Oh sure, you think you'll miss this place, and you probably will for a while. But you'll find new friends and you'll like your new school and neighborhood so much that you won't even remember this place after awhile. And it's fun to move into a new house. You'll see.'

"So they found a new house and they moved, and the moving was fun. The children enjoyed exploring the new house. But somehow Paula was still worried about the new school. She didn't know if the other children would like her.

"Well, that's where I ended, boys and girls. Anyone have any ideas about what Paula can do so that when she comes to the new school the children will like her and she can be happy?"

"Maybe she could bring some good toys to school, and then the other kids would want to play with her."

"She could have a party and invite the kids."

"The teacher could tell the other kids to be nice to her."

"And the teacher could tell the new girl to be nice to the other kids and then they'd like her."

"How do you think it feels to be a new child in school?" Mr. Clancy asked the class.

"You might feel scared at first. Because you don't know anybody."

"Yeah, everybody else knows the kids, but you don't. I remember that when I moved here last year."

"Can the children in the class do anything to make the new person feel comfortable?" wondered Mr. Clancy.

"They could tell the girl their names, so she'd know them."

"They could ask her to play with them."

"Yeah, and they could show her the things in the room."

"We have a number of ideas. Perhaps some of you can show us what you would do to help a new person feel at home. Let's see, we might have two old-timers, and the new girl. Who would like to be Paula?" asked Mr. Clancy as he moved into role playing with the class. "Jane can take the part of Paula and she'll come in the door and I'll introduce her to the class and ask Jeff and Sue to particularly help her for the day. Let's start. . . ."

ANALYSIS   This teacher is going to use role playing to help children with a situation which has not yet arisen. Before he begins the actual role playing he asks some questions designed to evoke pupil conversation and thought about the situation. What kinds of episodes might fruitfully be role played in classrooms at what grade level?

SKILL SESSION   Role play the situation being discussed in this situation. Have several groups role play in turn, and particularly observe the teacher's conversation after each session is completed. The teacher should show no preference for any group's ideas or actions, but should accept each contribution and move on. Each role playing episode may be ended by the teacher at the point he thinks best, but the cut-off should not imply that the role playing was not fruitful.

Situation 5

"I'd like to talk with you about all the tattling that's been going on lately in this class," said Mrs. Larkin to her fourth graders. "It seems that every five minutes someone comes up to complain to me about what somebody else is doing. It's 'Ina is copying my paper,' or 'Andy took my pencil,' or 'Mike pushed Rita,' or 'Ora didn't do her work.' Now what can we do about this? I don't like to constantly hear such tales."

"Well some kids *are* always copying."

"That's right. They always want to look at your paper."

"I didn't mean to say that I think you make up the things you tell me. I know that sometimes children copy and take pencils and push each other. But I wondered if there wasn't some other way we might handle these things. Do you think that you should come up to tell me about all of these things?" asked Mrs. Larkin.

"Well, the teacher has to know who's bad."

"You think the teacher should know about the children who misbehave?" asked Mrs. Larkin.

"Sure. Otherwise they'll just get away with it. The teacher should make the kids act good."

"And how will the teacher do that?" Mrs. Larkin inquired.

"She should tell the kids to stop what they're doing."

"You have to make them give the pencil back, or do their work, or stop pestering. Whatever they're doing you should tell them the right thing."

"Are there ever times when children should try to solve things by themselves?" asked Mrs. Larkin.

"Not in school. You should always tell the teacher."

"After school you can do what you want, but in school you have to tell."

"My mother tells us not to tattle. She don't want to hear about it."

"Mine says there's two sides to every argument."

"Can children ever learn anything from trying to settle their own arguments and problems?" asked Mrs. Larkin.

"Well, they might."

"What can they learn?" was Mrs. Larkin's next question.

There was a period of silence, but finally one child said, "Well, they can learn to settle their fights by themselves."

"And is that important to learn?" asked Mrs. Larkin.

"Yes—because you might not always have a teacher around."

"So it's important for children to learn to solve problems because the teacher or other adults might not be around. And of course, children grow up and become the adults, and then it's certainly important for them to know how to solve their problems. Now," continued Mrs. Larkin, "are there some things that happen here in school that are so important that you should come and tell me right away?"

"Sure. Like if somebody was going to throw a rock on the playground or something like that."

"You're saying that if something really dangerous is going to happen, it's important to come and tell me about it."

"Yes, if somebody would get hurt, we should tell you."

"Now, how can you decide when something is important enough for you to report it to me?"

"You have to think about it, and if it's important you would tell."

"Can you give me some examples of things you might tell me and things you wouldn't bother to tell me?"

"You shouldn't tell the teacher just because somebody pushes."

"Yeah—well you're always pushing, so that's why you say that."

"How about if someone doesn't do his school work? Should you tell me about that?"

"Well, school work is important."

"Do I have to know right away about that? Or will I find out when I look over everyone's work?"

"Well, you'll find out, so it's not important to tell right away."

"How about copying? Should you tell me about that?"

"That's not dangerous, so you don't have to know."

"But they shouldn't copy. It's not fair."

"Sometimes I notice that you children complain if someone copies your drawing. I really don't think that's very serious. In fact, I should think you'd be pleased if someone thought your picture was so good that he wanted to try to do something like it. And if anybody looks at your paper because he doesn't know an answer, I think that I usually see that. Even if I don't it's probably best if you don't tell me about it. Perhaps a good rule will be just to say that if it's really important, for instance if it's dangerous, you should tell me. But if it's just sort of annoying or bothersome, for instance if someone is whispering, then we won't say anything. And if people are pushing, and it isn't very serious, they can probably work it out by themselves. Anyway, let's try this rule for awhile, and see what happens."

ANALYSIS Analyze the interaction in this situation by referring to the VICS categories. Are any categories missing?

SKILL SESSION Practice your verbal behavior by taking each pupil statement in this situation which shows feeling (and most of them do) and accepting it in the three ways discussed in situation 1 of this section. The three methods of acceptance were identification, objective reflection, and giving evidence of listening with interest.

Discuss when it is appropriate to use these three methods of acceptance by applying them to the following examples:

1. I don't like you.

2. This math is too hard.

3. This is my new dress.

4. I lost a library book.

5. I like him.

6. I bumped my knee and it hurts.

7. Then she told me her side, but I didn't believe it.

8. I'll never learn to speak French.

9. When he says that I always get mad.

10. She said she didn't do it, so then I felt better.

Situation 6

Mr. Jeffries was speaking to his fifth grade class. "I think we need to talk about this homework situation. More and more I find that people are not finishing their assignments, and are handing in messy papers. Naturally, that's not everyone—there are still many who do their work well and faithfully. But more and more of you do not. Now, what's the reason?"

When no one responded Mr. Jeffries continued, "I'm really interested in knowing why. I think we can discuss it openly. Perhaps you think you have too much homework. If you think that, don't be afraid to say so."

There was another silence, but Mr. Jeffries waited without speaking. Finally one child began, "I think it's too much. When I come home from school I like to have some time to play outside before dinner."

"Me too. And I have to practice the piano, besides. Then, after I do my homework I never even have time to watch TV."

"And I have to go to religious school, so I never have enough time."

"And dancing school."

"So, many of you have a variety of things to do after school," summarized Mr. Jeffries, "—lessons, plus homework, plus the fact that you want to watch some programs, and you want to have some time to play."

"And besides that I have to help set the table and do the dishes."

"Me too."

"And, in addition to all the other things, you have chores to do. So—what's the solution?" asked Mr. Jeffries.

"Not so much homework," came the almost unanimous response from the class, though a few were heard to say, "*No* homework."

"But what do you think is most important in your lives—learning, or playing and watching TV?" was Mr. Jeffries' next question.

"Learning," said some resigned voices.

"Exactly! Now all of you are old enough to see that, I'm sure. Certainly we don't want to cut down on our homework! We just need to concentrate a little harder, perhaps, and spend our time more carefully, and then I'm sure we'll be able to fit everything in. Now, let's keep that in mind and see if we don't improve our work. I'm glad we had this little discussion to clear the air. I think we were all helped by it. Now, let's get on with our work for the day."

ANALYSIS   When you analyze this situation using the VICS you will notice that the teacher accepts the pupils' feelings up to a certain point in the discussion, and then he asks a narrow question—one to which the pupils know society's expected answer. Then, with his next statement he rejects all of the pupils' feelings which had been expressed earlier about too much homework.

SKILL SESSION   Modify the teacher talk in this situation so that the final outcome of the case is different.

Situation 7A

Mrs. Hatfield had asked Rita Barrett, a youngster in her sixth grade class, to have a conference with her, because she was concerned about the fact that the girl was so quiet and withdrawn. She never volunteered in any discussion, she seemed to have no friends, she sought out no one, and she was sought by no one.

"I asked you to stay and talk with me, Rita, because I'm a bit concerned about you. You never speak in class unless I call upon you, even though I know that you always have the answers. Why don't you join in more?"

"I don't know, Mrs. Hatfield. I guess I just don't talk very much."

"But you do listen to the discussion, don't you?"

"Yes."

"And you do know the answers. Whenever I call on you, you answer well, and your tests show good work."

"Well, I guess I know the answers."

"Then why don't you speak up more? It would be good for you, and you would help the class. I think you would make more friends if you spoke up too. What do you think?"

"I guess you're right."

"Well, I'm glad you agree. Then, from now on you're going to join in more often and not be so shy."

"Well—I'll try."

"Good. That's settled. Thank you for talking with me, dear."

ANALYSIS   This teacher attempts to build the confidence of a student in her class by trying to reassure her that she is a capable student.

Notice that the teacher praises the youngster, but uses no acceptance of what the youngster says. Acceptance of what a person actually says, or of the feelings behind the statement, is probably one of the best ways to reassure a person and let him know that we are genuinely interested in him. We often tend to try to reassure people by giving them information or opinion or direction, but this is not necessarily helpful. Praise may not be reassuring either, if the person is trying to say that he's worried, or that he doesn't feel sure of himself. What we may do when we give information, opinion, direction, or praise is cut the person off by saying (without meaning to) "I am not really interested in your feelings or what you are trying to tell me."

SKILL SESSION   Modify each of the teacher's statements in this situation so that they will encourage the pupil to talk.

Role play this same conference, with the person playing the role of the teacher attempting to encourage the pupil to talk as much as possible. Several persons might role play this in turn before the class, or the class might divide into groups of two or three (the third person being the observer) and take turns with the various roles.

Situation 7B

Mrs. Thatcher was concerned about Diane Jefferson, because she was so quiet and withdrawn. She never volunteered in her sixth grade class, and she seemed to have no friends. Mrs. Thatcher arranged to have a conference with the girl.

"I asked you to stay and talk with me, Diane, so that we could get to know each other a bit better. You know that I've been having conferences with some of the children, and I usually try to get to everybody. Tell me—how do you think your work is going?"

"All right."

"You did very well in the science quiz. In fact, you do well in all of your written work. You're a good student."

"Oh—I don't know."

"What are your favorite subjects?"

"Oh—I like everything. I guess maybe I like reading best."

"I've been noticing, Diane, that you hardly ever raise your hand in class. When I call on you, you answer well, and you really help us out. You know, the more people contribute to class discussions, the better the discussions usually are."

"Well, a lot of times I'd like to join in. But—I don't know. I guess I'm shy or something."

"I think many people feel that way. You know, I take a course on Tuesday nights over at the college, and I'm the same way. I have to *make* myself talk—and then I always wonder if it wouldn't have been better if I'd kept still!"

"That's the way I feel! After I say something, I think it sounds dumb."

"I wonder why so many of us feel that way? But, what you have to say, Diane, is always so thoughtful. You *certainly* never sound dumb. Do you mind being called on?"

"Yes, sometimes. But I really don't. I don't know—I do and I don't."

"Well, I was going to suggest that in order to get you started, I ought to call on you a bit more than I do. How would that be?"

"Well—all right," Diane agreed hesitantly.

"And, Diane, I'm thinking of asking you to be on the committee to plan our parent day program. I think you'd be a big help. What do you say?"

"Well, I don't know. I guess it's okay."

"Fine. And why don't we have another conference next week to see how things are going? Thank you for talking with me, Diane."

ANALYSIS Identify the statements with which Mrs. Thatcher, the teacher in this situation, accepts the feelings of the pupil.

Describe some of the feelings which are probably behind this pupil's statements.

SKILL SESSION Modify this teacher's verbal behavior so that she accepts all of the feelings which the pupil in the situation seems to be expressing.

Situation 7C

Mrs. Cullen was concerned about Inez Black, one of her sixth graders, and she decided to have a conference with the girl. Inez never spoke in class unless called upon, and she appeared to have no friends among the other children.

"You know, Inez, that I've been having conferences with some of the children—just to get to know everyone as well as I can. Now, why don't you tell me a bit about yourself—what you like about our class, and what you don't like about it."

"Well, I like it."

Mrs. Cullen said, "I see," and then waited until Inez continued.

"I guess I like some parts better than others. I like reading."

"Um hum," said Mrs. Cullen.

"And I like when we write poems and stories. And I like social studies."

"Are there some parts you don't like?" asked Mrs. Cullen.

"I don't think so. I really like everything. Well, I don't like current events too much." Inez paused for awhile. "I don't like it when it's my turn."

"You feel uncomfortable about talking in front of the class."

"Yes, I feel kind of funny. I like to listen to the other kids, though. It's really interesting. But I don't think what I say is too good."

"You think that some of the other children have better current events reports."

"Well, a lot of the other kids can just say their reports. I always read mine, and it's not so interesting. But I don't want to make any mistakes, so I don't want to just talk. That's why I read all my reports."

"Reading the reports does make us feel more secure."

"Well, I don't want to sound dumb or anything like that."

Mrs. Cullen said nothing, and after about thirty seconds Inez continued. "I *never* talked much in school. I usually know the answers, but I don't like to raise my hand. I'd rather have tests."

There was another pause, and Mrs. Cullen said, "I see."

"Sometimes, though, I'd like to give answers," Inez continued. "But I never raise my hand anyway. I don't know why."

"When I call on you your answers are always helpful, Inez. And your test papers and stories are interesting too. You're a good student, you know."

"Well, I'm not as good as Jean or Quentin. They always raise their hands and what they say is always good."

"You feel that they are better students."

"Yes. I could never be like them. I can't talk like that. I guess I'm too bashful. That's what everybody in my family always says—that I'm shy. But I do talk at home. It *would* be good to talk more in class." There was a pause before Inez went on, "Today I wanted to tell about a book I read over the weekend, when we were talking about how we spent our time. I read a book about some kids who find a deserted island, and they keep it a secret from everybody, and they build a cabin there and everything. It was really good."

"That does sound like a good story. You read a lot of books, I gather."

"Yes, I love to read. I go to the library about three times a week, and I think I've read practically everything there by now. The librarian is my friend. She lets me help her sometimes. I'm going to be a librarian when I grow up."

"You know, Inez, now that I know that you're so keen on books, and that you know about libraries, I have an idea. Our school library is kind of a mess, and at our last staff meeting we talked about re-cataloging the books and putting different cards in them, so that we'll have a better borrowing system. If you would be willing, I think you could be a great help. Not everyone likes to read, you know, but books are important, and the more we can get everyone in our school to want to read, the better. What do you think?"

"Oh, I'd like to help, Mrs. Cullen. The librarian at the public library lets me put the books away on the shelves sometimes, and I know a lot about libraries. I even know how to stamp the books to go out."

"Wonderful. There's quite a bit to do, of course, so you'll need to work with one or two of the other children. Tomorrow and the next day I'll give you some time to look over the library. Then in two or three days we can have another meeting and think about who else might be on this library committee. Perhaps you'll have some names to suggest."

"Okay."

"I'm certainly glad we had this chance to talk, Inez. See you in the morning."

ANALYSIS How does each teacher's verbal behavior in situations 7A, 7B, and 7C directly lead to the verbal behavior of the three pupils involved?

Classify the accepting statements of the teacher in situation 7C according to whether she uses identification, objective reflection, or just indicates that she is listening (see situation 1 in this section).

Find the teacher's statement of praise in situation 7C and notice the pupil's response.

SKILL SESSION   Divide into groups of two and talk to each other about the greatest problem you have or think you will have in teaching. Practice pausing, and sometimes wait up to thirty seconds before you comment or respond to your partner. Try also to accept what your partner says.

How did you *feel* during the periods of silence?

Situation 8

One day Mrs. Overholt found one of the seventh grade girls crying in the locker room. "Why, Ann, what's wrong?" she asked, putting her arm around the girl's shoulder. "Why are you crying?"

"I don't know," Ann replied tearfully.

"But you must be crying about something. If you tell me, perhaps I can help you."

"Nobody can help," said Ann, trying to dry her eyes. "It's just that some of the girls were talking about going to Carol's party, and what they were going to wear, and stuff like that."

"And you weren't invited."

"No."

"Then you feel quite left out."

"I'm always left out!" was Ann's vehement response. "They're always having parties and doing things and they never ask me. Just because they have more money. It's not fair. I'm just as good as they are."

"Well—things can't really be that bad, Ann. Try to look at the bright side of things."

"But things *are* that bad. And there isn't any bright side!" blazed Ann, beginning to cry again.

Mrs. Overholt patted the youngster's shoulder, feeling helpless. What could she do? She couldn't tell the others to include Ann in after-school activities.

"I guess maybe things are pretty bad, at that, Ann. And all I can do is say I'm sorry. Come on we'll have to get your face washed because they'll be locking up soon," she said as she walked with Ann toward the washroom.

ANALYSIS   Analyze this situation by describing the talk, using the VICS categories.

Can this teacher do anything besides say, "I'm sorry,"? Does she accomplish anything positive? *Can* teachers do anything in school to overcome the kind of problem this youngster has outside of school?

SKILL SESSION   Break into groups of two and role play other possible endings, beginning with the youngster's statement, "But things *are* that bad. And there isn't any bright side!"

Compare the endings of the different groups after the role-playing session.

Situation 9

"It's time to get ready for music," Mr. Kronfield announced to his eighth grade homeroom class, to the accompaniment of groans and complaints.

"Not again." "Why do we have to have music twice a week?" "Ugh—Mrs. Turner." These were some of the comments as the class put their books into their desks.

"I take it that music is not one of your favorite subjects," commented Mr. Kronfield.

"You said it!"

"There *is* one that's better—detention," said one of the boys as the others laughed.

"I should think you'd enjoy singing," said Mr. Kronfield.

"Well, we wouldn't mind singing. But we hardly ever sing. And when we do, you should hear the songs she picks!"

"Yeah—they're the worst, man."

"Mostly all we do is sing phrases for her, while she gives us marks in her book."

"And it's so boring that everybody else gets silly, and then she starts yelling."

"So it isn't that you don't like music or singing, but that you don't like it this year, is that right? Have you ever spoken to Mrs. Turner about your feelings?"

"Are you kidding?"

"That's all we need!"

"Well, I don't mean to tell her so that she'll be offended. But perhaps you could suggest some songs to her that you'd like to sing."

"Not with Mrs. Turner!"

"Why don't you ask her for us, Mr. Kronfield?"

"Well, I don't want to interfere with her work. She's a specialist in music, and I don't know much about her subject. I don't think I'd be too happy if she came in and tried to tell me about how to teach my math classes. But maybe I could find a way to tactfully mention to her that some of you had certain songs that you liked very much, that you particularly wanted her to teach to the class. Tomorrow I'll ask you for the names of a few songs, and then I'll see what I can do. Now it's time to go—and if you behave well for the next few days she may be more apt to listen to your request."

ANALYSIS   Which pupil statements does this teacher accept, and which does he respond to with other VICS categories?

SKILL SESSION   Role play a situation in which pupils complain about another teacher's homework assignments, saying that they are too long and are not helpful. The teacher should try to communicate any feelings of discomfort he has about his role in a discussion involving another teacher, but should try to accept the children's feelings.

Is it possible for teachers to accept pupils' feelings about other teachers without being unprofessional?

Situation 10

"Well, I don't like school anyway, so I don't care if I don't pass."

"Me neither. I'm quittin' as soon as I'm old enough."

"Yeah—you don't learn nothin' in school anyway—so who cares. I'm goin' out and earn some money and do what I want. Who cares about teachers anyway. They don't help you none, and they don't care about you. All they want to do is show you how dumb you are and how smart they are."

Mr. Massey had started this outburst in the ninth grade study hall by telling the youngsters to calm down and use the time to study—adding that if they didn't study they wouldn't pass.

"Well, you may think you want to get out and get a job now, but if you don't finish high school, you won't get a good job," Mr. Massey responded to the youngsters' arguments. "You should know that by now."

"Whaddya mean? I know a kid who makes a hundred dollars a week, and he didn't go to no high school."

"Yeah, and what about all them singers. They make plenty of money, and I know a lot of them don't finish school."

"And fighters, and ball players and things. They make money. A lot more than teachers."

"Well, you may be able to think of some examples of people who have good jobs, even though they didn't finish high school, but they are the exception," declared Mr. Massey. "All the statistics show that the more education you have, the higher your salary will be."

"Well, I don't believe it."

"Yeah—there's a guy on our block went to college, and he don't have *no* job. How do you like that!"

"It doesn't matter what you say. Education will help you, if you will only study and take it seriously. If you don't want to, that's your business. But in the meantime, I want all of you to be quiet so that people who do want to study can do so. And that's enough talk," Mr. Massey ended the discussion.

ANALYSIS   Describe the interaction in this situation by referring to the categories in the VICS. You will see that this teacher makes no attempt to accept these pupils' ideas or feelings, but does try to convince them that education will help them. Why do you think it is that people so often try to convince other people by rejecting their expression of feelings and their ideas, and by arguing with them? What might this teacher accomplish if he encouraged the youngsters to express their ideas and feelings about school and accepted them? Is it likely that he can convince these pupils that school is important?

SKILL SESSION   Modify this teacher's responses so that he accepts what the pupils say, but let him express his own point of view to them.

SOME BRIEF EXAMPLES
OF CONTRASTING
COUNSELING SITUATIONS

The following short situations are presented as contrasting examples of how different teachers might handle the same behavior. In each pair of situations contrast the verbal behavior employed, and discuss the underlying assumptions of the two teachers and the consequences of their differing verbal behavior.

Situation A

"I'm going to throw my painting in the basket. It's terrible."

"Don't be silly. That's a nice picture," said the teacher.

"I hate it. It's ugly," and the child crumpled the picture and threw it away.

"We don't do that with our pictures. You won't be allowed to paint if you're going to waste paper."

"I'm not going to paint any more anyway. I can't make anything good."

"Well, if that's the way you feel, then find something else to do."

Situation AA

"I'm going to throw my painting in the basket. It's terrible."

"Sounds as if you don't like the picture you made this morning," said the teacher.

"It's scribble-scrabble."

"Sometimes when we feel that our pictures aren't good, we want to throw them away."

"I'm going to make another picture, anyway. Do you want this one?" and the child handed his painting to the teacher and walked back to the easel to paint again.

Situation B

A child came up to the teacher and asked, "Do you like me?"

"What a silly question! Of course I like you. I like everyone," replied the teacher. "Now go back to your chair, and don't worry about such things."

Situation BB

A child came up to the teacher and asked, "Do you like me?"

"Are you worried because you think I don't like you?"

"Sometimes you don't like me because I make noise."

"You feel that when I tell you to be more quiet, I don't like you."

"Well *I* like *you*."

"We do worry about whether or not people like us, don't we? I'm glad you like me—and you know what? *I* like *you* too. Knowing that people care about us is a nice feeling, isn't it?"

Situation C

"I don't think my Halloween costume is very good, do you?" a child asked her teacher.

"Why, I think it's lovely. It's very original."

"I hate it. It's junky."

"That's a foolish thing to say. It's a very nice costume."

"Well, I think it's icky. I don't think the parade will be any fun."

Situation CC

"I don't think my Halloween costume is very good, do you?" a child asked her teacher.

"You feel that your costume isn't nice enough?"

"Well, some of the other kids might have better ones."

"People do worry about whether or not they'll look as good as everyone else."

"Do you like my wand? I think the silver star is nice, don't you?"

"You look like a real fairy princess with that wand."

"I made that myself. I can hardly wait for the parade to start."

Situation D

"Do you think the fifth grade will like our play?"

"The main thing is that we worked hard, and we did our best," replied the teacher. "We hope that the other class will like the play, naturally, and that's why we invited them. But as I said, we have done our best and that's all we really should be concerned about."

Situation DD

"Do you think the fifth grade will like our play?"

"I guess we all feel kind of worried about how the play will go," replied the teacher.

"Yeah, what if I forget my lines?"

"Me too. What if I forget the lines or something like that?"

"I suppose everyone who's in a play begins to worry about what will happen when the play is actually performed," the teacher commented.

"I remember in the third grade we were in a play and I was so scared I had a stomach-ache."

"When we worry about things sometimes we actually become sick over them," said the teacher.

"Everybody feels scared when they're in plays and things."

"Yeah, that's why we feel nervous."

"I hope everybody likes us."

"We do feel nervous, and that's certainly common, because we want the audience to like what we've done. We worry about what other people think of us, don't we? But we've worked hard, and I'm pretty sure the other class will like our play," came the teacher's final remark.

Situation E

"I don't think my story is too good."

"Then maybe you better work a little more on it," said the teacher.

"But I finished it."

"Well it's probably fine. Read it to us and don't worry. Nobody is perfect."

Situation EE

"I don't think my story is too good."

"You feel that perhaps your story isn't good enough?" asked the teacher.

"Well, it might be good, but maybe some kids won't like it."

"Everyone feels sometimes that his work isn't as good as he wishes it were."

"Yeah, that's the way I am," said another child.

"Well, I'll read it anyway. You can see how it is."

"Fine. We'll all listen," said the teacher.

Situation F

"Do you think the tests will be hard?"

"I don't think so," replied the teacher. "We've prepared carefully for them, and I think we'll do well. There's nothing to worry about."

"But what if we don't do well?"

"Believe me, we have nothing to worry about. We'll be all right, and if we don't do well, at least we will have tried. Worrying won't help, so just relax and think of something else."

Situation FF

"Do you think the tests will be hard?"

"You feel kind of worried about the tests, I guess," responded the teacher.

"Yes. What if I don't do well? Maybe I won't pass or something."

"You're worried about failing," said the teacher.

"Oh, I guess I'll pass okay. And I did study."

"You think you'll be all right, then," the teacher said.

"Well, I've done a lot of studying. I think I'll be okay. I always worry about tests."

"A lot of people do, I guess," was the teacher's final comment.

Situation G

"I don't know what to do about my high school course. My mother wants me to sign up for the academic program, but I'm not sure if I should."

"Well, of course you should take the academic program," said the teacher. "What else would you take?"

"I don't know. That's the hardest program, and I'm not sure if I can do it."

"But that's ridiculous, Jane. Of course you can do it—a smart girl like you. Certainly you'll take the academic course, and you'll do well in it. Now don't even think about anything else."

"Well, I suppose I'd better sign up for that. I guess I don't have any choice, anyway."

Situation GG

"I don't know what to do about my high school course. My mother wants me to sign up for the academic program, but I'm not sure if I should."

"Do you think you might like another program?" asked the teacher.

"Well, the academic program is the hardest one, and I'm not sure whether or not I can do the work. Maybe I should take the general course."

"I guess you're a little worried about the academic program."

"Well, all the smartest kids will probably take that course, and maybe I won't do so well."

"We do feel worried about getting good grades if we think that everyone else in the class will be very smart. And you like to do well in school, don't you, Jane?"

"Yes. And my mother always wants me to get very good marks. I do now, but what if I don't when I get to high school?"

"Are you afraid that you won't please your mother?"

"Well, she's so fussy. But I suppose I could do the work. I want to go to college, and I know I should take the academic course for that."

"You think that perhaps you'll be okay in the academic program."

"I think so. If I try I'm pretty sure I'll be okay. Thanks for helping me."

ANALYSIS You will have seen that although the teacher in the first of each of these pairs of situations tries to support the pupil or pupils, the attempted reassurance is not necessarily successful. Each teacher's message is that there's nothing to worry about or that it's pointless to worry. Saying this often rejects the feelings expressed by pupils, because their comments are either ignored or rejected. These teachers are saying. "I won't listen to your feelings; they are not important; don't go on." Yet each teacher undoubtedly believes that he is using reassuring verbal behavior. Most people try to reassure others in this "there's nothing to worry about" manner, but it is often not the best approach.

Certain kinds of praise may actually produce defensive reactions on the part of the person being praised. If a youngster is feeling upset, angry, or otherwise defensive, then praise may have a negative effect upon him. And the more a child has met with rejection, the more defensive he will probably be, and the more unable he may be to accept the kind of praise which says, "You are competent, you have nothing to worry about."

Remember that acceptance of feeling is not synonymous with praise. Praise often ignores feeling completely, since it is usually directed toward behavior or ideas.

SKILL SESSION   React to the following statesments in two ways. First, try to reassure the speaker that "there's nothing to worry about." In the second instance, accept his feelings.

1. I might not be promoted.

2. I bet I won't make the team.

3. My dress isn't as nice as hers.

4. Do you think she likes me?

5. I'm afraid of the dark.

6. The paper I wrote isn't very good.

7. I never do anything right.

8. I might make a mistake when I'm on the stage.

9. How will I ever learn all this stuff?

SELECTED REFERENCE

HDI Program, *General Relationship Improvement Program,* 4th ed. Atlanta, Georgia: Human Development Institute, Inc., 1964.

CHAPTER 9

Evaluating

Two of the teaching activities defined in this book may be carried out as "teacher acts" as well as "teaching activities"—that is, they may be carried out apart from pupils. Planning is one of these, and evaluating the other. When teachers fill out report cards or write cumulative records, they are evaluating pupils, but they are not engaged in teaching *activities,* which means that they are not engaged interactively with pupils in the classroom.

Just as the goal in disciplining is pupil self-discipline, so the goal for sound evaluation should be realistic self-evaluation. If pupils are to evaluate themselves realistically they must have practice, and must share in the determined criteria. And when pupils evaluate experiences they have had, teachers must take care to permit honest evaluation.

Since the major job of the teacher is to help pupils learn, teacher evaluation should be given with this in mind. If the teacher's task is to help pupils, then evaluation must be helpful—it must lead to further learning, whether that learning be social, emotional or cognitive.

The situations, skill sessions, and analyses presented in the rest of this chapter were written to help you increase your evaluating skills; and remember, good intentions are not enough. Skill is needed, and skill requires examination, analysis and practice.

Situation 1A

Miss Dale began the discussion of a visit to the firehouse with her first grade class by saying, "We certainly had a good time at the firehouse yesterday. Let's spend some time today talking about what happened and what we have learned. Who would like to tell us something he particularly liked about the trip?"

"I'm gonna be a fireman."

"Me, too."

"So am I."

"You can't be—you're a girl."

"I wonder why so many of you want to be firemen?" asked Miss Dale.

"You get to ride fast on the truck."

"And because you can wear the hat and the boots."

"I want the axe."

"You can slide down the pole."

"And you can climb high ladders and you can use the hose."

"And," Miss Dale asked, "why would you like to do those things?"

"Because it's fun," came the answer.

"I guess it *would* be exciting to ride on the fast fire truck, and wear a fireman's uniform and all the other things you mentioned. And you know, another nice thing about being a fireman is that you have a chance to help people, and that's a good feeling to have about the work you do. Do any of you think that someday girls might be able to work as firemen?"

"Naw. You have to be a man."

"There's no girl firemen."

"You have to be strong."

"Well, a lot of jobs which used to be held only by men are now held by women. Did you know that?" asked Miss Dale. "At one time there were no women doctors or lawyers. And there weren't any policewomen, but you know that there are now because one visited us here in our classroom. So perhaps someday we will have firewomen —who knows. Women usually aren't as strong as men, but there might be some work they could do. Can you think of something that a firewoman could do?"

"Well, they could drive the truck. I saw a lady driving a truck once."

"All right. Now, do you remember that the fireman talked to us about fire prevention?" inquired Miss Dale.

"Yeah—I didn't like that."

"Me neither. I don't even know what he was talking about."

"That part was no good."

"Perhaps he did spend a bit long on that. You know, I think he may have thought you children were older than you really are, because you listened so quietly, and so he talked to you about things that were rather hard to understand. But really, all he was saying was that we need to be very careful about fire, and never play with matches or with the stove. Fire can be very dangerous and so it has to be used with great care.

"Now," continued Miss Dale, "what are some of the things we learned during our trip? Later on we'll write some of these things down, but for now let's just talk. Who wants to tell us something that he learned?"

"We learned the names of the different equipments."

"Yes, we learned about the equipment. Now, what were some of the things called that we saw and what were they used for? . . ."

ANALYSIS   Describe the talk in this situation using the VICS categories. What categories are missing? Notice that the teacher sometimes asks questions after children's contributions without responding first by accepting or rejecting their contributions. This is often a good way to encourage discussion. It is not necessary to comment directly on what pupils have said in order to encourage wide participation.

SKILL SESSION   Practice asking questions which are designed to encourage continued pupil talk after each of the following statements:

1. Policemen can help you if you're lost.

2. People should vote because it's their responsibility to help elect good leaders.

3. You give a letter to the post office, and then they deliver it.

4. That report was good because they worked so hard on it.

5. Storekeepers are important because they sell things that people need.

6. The colonies wanted to break away from the mother country because they didn't think they were being fairly represented.

7. If you can't do arithmetic, then you won't be able to buy things in a store.

Situation 1B

"Boys and girls," began Miss Hastings to her first grade class, 'I'd like to talk about the trip we made yesterday to the firehouse. First of all, let's list some of the things we particularly enjoyed. Who wants to begin?"

"I liked when the man slided down the pole. I want to do that."

"Me too."

"We say 'slid,' not 'slided,'" corrected Miss Hastings. "Suppose I write 'Things We Liked At The Firehouse' here on the board, and I'll put 'Watching the fireman slide down the pole' right under that. What else?"

"I liked when they let us ring the bell."

"All right. I'll put down, 'Ringing the fire truck bell.'"

"I liked the part when he let us sit up in the seat."

"Good. I'll write 'Sitting in the fire truck.' What else?"

"I'm going to be a fireman when I grow up."

"Me too."

"So am I."

"Wait a minute. Did you all raise your hands? And you aren't sticking to the topic. We're making a list of what we liked at the firehouse. Now pay attention. Anyone else have anything? How about the talk the fireman gave us about fire prevention. I'm sure we liked that. I'll put down, 'Learning about fire prevention.' Anyone else? Well, I think that's enough of a list. Now I'll put this on chart paper and we can read it over tomorrow and for the next few days. Let's look at the board now, and see how well we can read what we have written! Charles, will you start?"

ANALYSIS   Analyze this situation by using the VICS categories and compare the interaction with that in situation 1A.

What seems to be the major goal of the teacher in situation 1A? In situation 1B?

The teacher's verbal behavior in situation 1B is an example of how teachers can begin pupils on the road to discovering that teachers are often not really interested in hearing about the ideas and feelings which their classroom questions seem, on the surface, to call for.

SKILL SESSION   Change these evaluative teacher statements into broad evaluative questions using Gallagher and Aschner's definition of an evaluative question (see pages 26–28):

1. I'm sure we liked that.

2. We certainly had a good time, didn't we?

3. The early settlers were a brave and hardy lot.

4. That report was excellent.

5. If we don't listen, we won't learn.

6. Wasn't that a good story?

7. Don't you think you should add some brighter colors to that picture?

8. This experiment will be interesting.

9. Your behavior today was particularly good.

10. Spelling is important, so be sure to study your words well.

Situation 2A

Each of the reading groups in Mrs. Passman's second grade class had had its turn with her during the reading period, and now after the children had a brief game for relaxation she asked them to continue with their seat-work activities, while she took a few minutes to review the workbook assignments for the day with these groups which had had such work.

She began with one group by saying, "Let's all look at page 22. Loren, will you tell us what we were to do on this page?"

"We had to read the words in this column and then draw a line from a word here to a word in that column."

"Yes, we were to draw a line from the words in the left-hand column to the appropriate color words in the right-hand column. Now, let's check our work. Would you read the first word, Jean," requested Mrs. Passman, "and tell us which word you drew your line to."

"The word is 'cloud' and I drew the line to the color 'white.'"

"So the word is 'cloud' and we know that the color of clouds is usually white," said Mrs. Passman. "But let's look closely at that word 'white.' Some of you were caught on this one, because this page is tricky. I'm going to put 'white' and another word up here on the board. They look very much alike. Now—which one is 'white?' Yes, this one. And what does this other word say? Does anyone know?"

"While."

"Yes. Now, how can you tell which is which?"

"Because I hear the 't' in 'white,' and I hear the 'l' in 'while.'"

"Good. Does everyone hear that difference, and see the difference? 'White,' 'while,'" pronounced Mrs. Passman slowly, as she pointed to the words and their differences. "See how much they look alike, but how important the difference is. We have to be careful to look all the way across the word to be sure of what it says. Now that we've done this first one, take a few minutes to look carefully over your other words, because many of them look almost alike, and you have to be *very* careful not to be caught. I'll go to another group, and then come back to you when you've had time to check your work."

ANALYSIS   Usually children's answers contain something in them that is correct or logical. When giving corrective feedback, or leading children toward more appropriate responses, it may be helpful to accept that part of the child's statement which makes sense. For instance, if a child reads the word 'while' as 'white,' the teacher might say, 'These words do look quite a bit alike, but 'white' has one letter in it which 'while' does not. What is it?' and then lead the pupil to correct his own mistake. It is often good pedagogy to help a child correct his own error, instead of calling on another youngster who already knows the answer. In fact, calling on someone else may be harmful to the pupil who has made the error.

SKILL SESSION   Change the following teacher comments so that they accept what is logical in the pupil's statement, and then add statements that will help the child arrive at a more appropriate response, or explain the reasons for his response.

Pupil   That word is "Daddy."
Teacher   If you were looking, you would know it said "Father."

Pupil   Three times three is six.
Teacher   Who can help Jane?

Pupil   In summer the sun is closer to the earth.
Teacher   If you had read the chapter carefully you would not give the wrong answer.

Pupil   A rectangle is the same as a square.
Teacher   A square has four equal sides.

Pupil   To lecture is to scold someone.
Teacher   That's not what the word means here.

Pupil   I don't think Tim was happy.
Teacher   That's not right. The story tells us he was.

Pupil   There are twelve hours in a day.
Teacher   No. There are twenty-four hours in a day.

Situation 2B

Monday morning Mrs. Tilden passed back to her second graders the reading workbooks which she had collected from them on the previous Friday. She then assigned seat work for two reading groups and asked the third group to open their workbooks to page 22 so that they could look over what they had done.

"Many of you did poorly on these pages, and I don't know why. We went over everything beforehand, and you should have been able to do this work. You weren't paying close enough attention. I think that some of you think it's enough to just get through the pages. But it's important to get the answers right. Now look at page 22. You were supposed to draw the lines from the words in the left-hand column to the proper words in the right-hand column. What is the first word?"

"Cloud."

"And what are you supposed to draw the line to?" asked Mrs. Tilden.

"White."

"Yes. Not 'while' as many of you did, but 'white.' And the next word, 'sky.' Where should you draw the line?" When a child said "blue," Mrs. Tilden continued, "All right. Most of you had that one right. What about the word 'grass'?"

"Green."

"Yes, it should have been 'green,' not 'greed.' Many of you just aren't looking at the words. You know that grass is green. Now how about the next word, 'sun'. . . ."

ANALYSIS   Compare the interaction in this situation with that in situation 2B.

What assumptions do the teachers in these two cases seem to have about how children's work should be evaluated?

Notice that one teacher holds the evaluation session much sooner after the pupils' work is completed than the other. What effect do you think this will have on the improvement of the pupils' future work?

SKILL SESSION   Sometimes teachers will want to accept only part of a pupil's statement, and yet not reject the part which is incorrect.

For instance, a pupil might say, "Washington, D.C. is the capital of the United States and it is in Virginia." The teacher might respond by saying, "Washington *is* our capital. It's right on the border of the state of Virginia. Would you go to the map and trace the border of both Virginia and Maryland and tell us if Washington falls within the border of either of those states?"

Accept what is appropriate in the following pupil statements, without rejecting anything, and then help the child to a better response.

1. A quart is larger than a pint because it takes three pints to make a quart.
2. Four times six is ten.
3. Mothers don't have jobs. They stay home and work there.
4. New York is larger than Texas.
5. The moon is bigger than the planets.

Situation 3

Mr. Anson had passed the arithmetic tests back to his third grade class after correcting them. "Boys and girls, now that we have this test in front of us, I think we have a pretty good idea of how we are doing with the multiplication tables. What do you think? Do we need more practice, or are we ready to move on?"

"I need more practice."

"I know the tables now."

"I need more time on the sevens tables."

"I need practice on the nines."

"I want to do something else. I know these."

"Some people think they're ready to go on, and others want more time on the tables. I think we're going to have to split up for a while. How shall we work that out?" asked Mr. Anson.

"We could have all the sevens people in one place and the people who don't want help in another place, and the fives in a place, and like that."

"Good suggestion," agreed Mr. Anson. "Let's start by having the people who want more help come over into this part of the room. The rest of you move over to this side and I'll get you started on something else. While I do that, you other people can be studying your tables—you can use the buddy system if you are very quiet about it."

ANALYSIS   When the teacher in this situation asks children to evaluate their ability to handle the multiplication tables, they know that they can respond honestly and not be reprimanded. Why is it that so often when teachers ask such questions as, "Does everybody understand now?" children are reluctant to say that they need more help? Why do you think that teachers often make statements which discourage children from asking for aid, even though the primary task of the teacher is to help children learn?

SKILL SESSION   The following teacher statements probably discourage pupils from asking for help. Modify these statements so that children would feel very free to request needed assistance.

1. We'll have to move on now if we're going to cover everything.

2. No more time for questions. If you don't understand you'll have to listen more carefully in the future.

3. Now, if we've paid attention I'm sure we understand.

4. That chapter makes everything very clear.

5. We've gone over this so many times, I can't understand how there can still be questions.

6. If this class would listen more, there wouldn't be so much need to ask for help.

Situation 4

"How would you say you behaved in the lunchroom today?" Mrs. Thornton asked her third grade class.

"Terrible. Some kids were awful noisy."

"Yeah, and Johnny rolled an egg up and down the table."

"Mr. Carey had to yell at us three times, and he made some kids stay in after they were through."

"Now why do you think this is happening?" asked Mrs. Thornton.

"Well, I didn't do anything. Me and Mary Jane were quiet."

"I didn't do nothing either. Some of the kids are noisy, but not everyone."

"But when Mr. Carey reports your behavior, he doesn't say 'some children'; he says to me, 'Mrs. Thornton, your *class* was very noisy today.' Because as far as he is concerned our whole table is noisy. Now what can we do about it?"

"Well, we should be quiet."

"Why should we be quiet?" inquired Mrs. Thornton.

"Because the lunchroom gets to sound terrible and it's not nice to eat in so much noise."

"You can always *say* the reasons why you should be quiet during lunchtime. But you continue to be noisy. Now why is this?" asked Mrs. Thornton.

"Because it's fun to make noise sometime."

"Who wants to be quiet all the time!"

"Well, I guess it is fun for children to make noise sometime. But you just *can't* continue to make noise in the lunchroom. None of our past resolutions have worked, so this time I'm going to suggest a different seating arrangement, and make an absolute rule that you can talk only to the people on each side of you, and then only in a very soft voice. Now let's work out the arrangement of who will sit next to whom. I'll let you help plan it out, but if this doesn't work, I won't consult you next time—and we'll have to have much more drastic measures."

ANALYSIS   Analyze the talk in this situation by referring to the VICS categories. Find examples of acceptance followed by rejection in this evaluation session.

SKILL SESSION   Role play a classroom session in which the teacher and children decide who will sit next to whom in the lunchroom, and why. Assign certain characteristics to some of the pupils—one who talks a great deal, someone who is silly, someone who is quiet, and so forth.

Situation 5A

"I have the spelling tests from yesterday to give back to you," declared Mrs. Travers to her fourth grade class, "so put away your reading books while I give them out. Let's see how we've done now. Raise your hand to show how many you have right. All right? One wrong? Two wrong? Three? Four? Five? More than five? Now, let's go over the words. Walt, you spell the first word for us. And listen carefully, boys and girls, so that you will learn the right way."

"Something, s-o-m-t. . . ."

"Wrong. If you had studied harder and paid more attention you wouldn't be constantly making mistakes. I've told you that over and over again. Chris, you spell that word for us."

"Something, s-o-m-e-t-h-i-n-g."

"Good. Chris pays attention, Walt, and that's why he has it right. Next word, Ida," requested Mrs. Travers.

"Really, r-e-a-l-y."

"No. Ida, you're another person who continually misspells the words, week after week. When you should be studying your words you just dream or fool around. Who can spell that one properly for us? . . ."

ANALYSIS   Describe the talk in this situation by referring to the categories in the VICS.

How do you think children feel about this kind of teacher?

What effect do you think a teacher's evaluation of a pupil's work has on the pupil when the evaluation is public; for instance, when children are asked how many words they have right, or what grades they received, or how many books they have read so far? Might this cause children to cheat? How can teachers help children to improve their work without holding up other pupils as examples of behavior to emulate or shun?

SKILL SESSION   Change the teacher statements in this situation to remove the rejection from them, and make them into helping statements.

Situation 5B

Mrs. Quentin had just finished dictating the spelling words for Group One's weekly test in her fourth grade. "Now let's see how we've done. Mary, will you please pass out the red pencils for marking, and let's put all other pens and pencils away. Who would like to spell the first word for us while I put them on the board? Ben?"

"Nothing, n-o-t-h-i-n-g."

"Good. Check your paper now and if you didn't spell the word correctly, write the proper spelling beside the word with your red pencil. Next, Tom," said Mrs. Quentin as she continued to call on children whose hands were raised.

"Anything, a-n-y-t-h-i-n-g."

"Fine. Harriet."

"Something, s-o-m-t-h-i-n-g."

"That's close, but you've left out one letter. I noticed as I walked around that several of you made the same error. Harriet, how is 'some' spelled?"

"Oh! Something, s-o-m-e-t-h-i-n-g."

"Yes. I think many of you were thinking of dropping the 'e' as we do in 'ing' words," noted Mrs. Quentin. "But in this case we keep the 'e.' Next, Ollie."

"Everything, e-v-e-r-y-t-h-i-n-g."

"Good. Marion, will you be next?"

When the children had finished reviewing their work, Mrs. Quentin said, "Let's take a moment to look over our papers. I see that many of us have done extremely well. If you missed any words add them to next week's list so that you can study them again. You people are really advancing in your spelling ability—and it shows in your stories and your other written work. All right, now—Jack will you collect the red pencils? I'll take the papers to look over, and you'll have them back tomorrow."

ANALYSIS What seem to be this teacher's assumptions about the role of pupils in the evaluative process? Compare the assumptions of the teacher in this situation with those of the teacher in situation 5A about the purpose of evaluation. What *is* the primary purpose in evaluating children's work or behavior? What role should children play in the evaluation process?

SKILL SESSION Sometimes teachers give children directions which they know the children can carry out, or which they know children like to carry out. At other times, teachers may direct children to do things which they cannot do, or do not want to do. Compare the directions given by the two teachers in situations 5A and 5B and change any directions given by either teacher which you think could be stated in more helpful form.

Situation 6

As they walked to school together a group of Mr. Norton's fourth graders discussed the report cards they would receive that day.

"I wonder if I'll be promoted."

"I hope I will be."

"Last time I got all A's and one B. I wonder what I'll get this time."

"I got an A in English all year. Maybe I'll get A again."

"I hope I get A in arithmetic again."

"He keeps giving me C in arithmetic, but I don't think it's fair. I do as good as plenty of other kids."

"My mother said if I get a good report, she'll get me a surprise."

"I hate report cards. I never do good in anything."

"Me neither. Hey, there's the bell," and the group ran into the school.

Later that morning, as Mr. Norton gave out the report cards he said, "The marks on these cards are *yours*—you have earned them. I'm sure you all know what you deserve, so let's take what we get like good sports. And there's no need to compare with anyone else. Just take them home with you, and let's have no fuss."

ANALYSIS   It is not uncommon for children to be unaware of the quality of their own work until an appraisal is forthcoming from the teacher. Often pupils are given no tools, no methods for evaluating their own efforts. In fact, youngsters often think that the reason for doing well is to please adults.

Many pupils never learn that achievement can bring satisfaction for the self, but learn only of the satisfaction which comes from adult approval or peer admiration. They learn that evaluation is not something which has to do with appraisal of self, but rather is something which adults give according to certain criteria which they do not readily share with pupils.

And, unfortunately, many children never even have the satisfaction of receiving adult approval *or* peer admiration in their school lives, because they do not achieve at a level which teachers regard as worthy of positive recognition.

SKILL SESSION   What are some questions which teachers might ask of children to encourage them to evaluate their own work realistically?

Suggest some questions that teachers might ask to encourage children to express their feelings about grades they have received? As you ask these questions keep in mind that teachers should be willing to modify the curriculum according to the composition of the class and its individual members.

Situation 7

It was ten minutes before the dismissal bell, and Mr. Blair and his fifth grade class usually spent this time looking back over the day's happenings.

"Who has something to say about today's activities?" asked Mr. Blair.

"I don't think everybody should have to play with the other kids at recess time. Me and Jane don't like to play softball or those games. We'd rather play jump-rope or something like that, and not have to do what everybody does," said Myra.

"But if everybody doesn't play then we never have enough for the game," countered Bill.

"Besides, some people don't have anything to do, and who wants to just run around. I like it when everybody plays the same thing," came from Elena.

"Well, I don't," Adam disagreed. "We could play marbles if we didn't have dodge ball and those things."

"Can anyone suggest a compromise? Something that will satisfy both those who want free play and those who want group play?" inquired Mr. Blair.

"Why don't we have everybody together in group games one week, and the next week everybody could do what they want," suggested Ross.

"Or we could have organized things on Monday, Wednesday, and Friday, and free play on Tuesday and Thursday," said Bill.

"Both of these suggestions would help us. Ross, your idea will take care of each side, and perhaps having both activities within one week as Bill suggests will provide more variety. I see a lot of heads nodding agreement. All right then," Mr. Blair continued, "we'll see how that plan works. Now *I'd* like to bring something up for discussion. And that is the way we're behaving during arithmetic group time. You know we've spoken about talking with someone if it's absolutely essential and if you can keep your voice to a whisper. Those whispers are getting awfully loud. What seems to be the problem?"

"Willie is always talking, and not about his work either. And he bothers me and I can't work," complained Ada. "He fools around too much."

"I do not," reacted Willie. "But sometimes I finish everything and there's nothing to do."

"What are we supposed to do if we finish our assigned work? Willie, can you read that chart up there as a reminder," requested Mr. Blair.

Willie read,

WHEN YOU FINISH YOUR WORK

Read a library book. Study your spelling words. Write a story.
Pick a work paper from the grab bag. Draw a picture.

"But I'm tired of those things," Willie remarked.

"I'm sorry if you're tired of them, Willie, but you must be quiet anyway. We don't have time right now, but perhaps we do need to come up with some new ideas for things to do when our work is finished," Mr. Blair speculated. "Let's speak about that in the morning. However, I want everyone to keep talk down to an absolute minimum during arithmetic time, and the level of talk must not be above a low whisper. Now, the bell's going to ring in three minutes, so let's get ready for home."

ANALYSIS   Analyze the interaction in this situation by referring to the VICS categories. Does the teacher use any rejecting statements?
What do you think of the idea of evaluating the school day with pupils?

SKILL SESSION   Notice that in this situation there is some pupil-to-pupil interaction after the teacher speaks. Teachers are often in the habit of speaking after each pupil speaks, and this is a difficult habit to break. However, if one considers it to be important for pupils to interact with each other, then the habit can be ended.
Role play a situation in which the teacher does not speak until at least two pupils have spoken. This may mean that there will be periods of silence. The teacher might announce

to the group that in order to encourage more pupil participation, he will not speak until at least two pupils have spoken. For the content of the discussion perhaps you might evaluate a trip to a bottling plant or to the post office, or you might evaluate a music period or any school activity, or you might want to evaluate the class in which you are currently participating.

Situation 8A

Mr. Smolen passed out a test to his fifth grade class and said, "Now let's read over the questions together to be sure that there's no doubt about what they say. We've discussed all of these things in class, and you should know the answers. Grace, will you read the first two."

" '1. Who debated against Lincoln in a famous series of debates before the Civil War? 2. Where was John Brown's raid?' "

"Good. Any questions about those? Next two, Hank."

" '3. What started the Civil War? 4. Who was the most famous Southern general?' "

"Fine. Any questions? Next two, Alice."

" '5. Which side had more people and wealth? 6. Which side hoped Britain would intervene in her favor?' "

"All right. Next two, Chris."

" '7. Who won the battle between the Monitor and the Merrimac? 8. How long did the Civil War last?' "

"Good. Last two, Heidi."

" '9. Where did the surrender take place? 10. In what year did the Civil War end?' "

"Good. Now are there any questions about this test? Then we can begin."

ANALYSIS You will notice that all the questions asked by this teacher are classified as cognitive memory questions according to the Gallagher and Aschner system (see pages 26–28). What is actually evaluated when these kinds of questions are asked?

SKILL SESSION Take each question asked by the teacher in this situation and modify it so that it falls into one of the three other Gallagher and Aschner categories.

Situation 8B

"Let's read over the test questions to be sure that everyone understands them. Some deal with things we've discussed in class, but some will cause you to do some new thinking, I hope," said Mr. Ponti to his fifth grade class. "Gus, would you read the first question."

" '1. What were some of the causes of the Civil War?' "

"I have a question about that," said one of the children. "Shall we just list causes, or shall we discuss them?"

"You don't have to discuss them," replied Mr. Ponti. "Just put down some of the reasons which resulted finally in the Civil War." The teacher looked around to see if anyone had further questions and then asked another child to read the next question.

" '2. What were some of the reasons why the North won and the South was defeated in the Civil War?' "

"Any problems about that one? Again—you won't discuss the reasons. Next question, Mildred."

" '3. Why is it sometimes said that both sides lose in every war?' "

"All right up to here?" asked Mr. Ponti. "Now notice that you have a choice in answering the next two questions. You can take *either* 4a or 4b."

"You mean everybody has to answer questions 1, 2, and 3; but we only take one out of 4a or 4b?"

"Right. So you'll all have only four answers, in all, on your papers. Arthur, will you read 4a and 4b?"

" '4a. How might our country be different now if the South rather than the North had won the Civil War? 4b. Suggest some steps that might have been taken to prevent the Civil War from ever being fought.' "

"Any questions? Well, if there are any as you go along, I'll be right up here. Now let's get started."

ANALYSIS   Analyze the questions asked by Mr. Ponti, the teacher in this situation, using the Gallagher and Aschner categories. Compare what it is that Mr. Ponti tries to evaluate with what Mr. Smolen, the teacher in situation 8A, attempts to evaluate.

SKILL SESSION   Give some information about the Civil War, or any other topic, and then develop a narrow question from that statement. Then go on to develop a broad question from the very same statement. For example, a teacher might give the following information:

"Some of the Indians in the United States build their homes from adobe, some from skins, and some from logs." He then might ask this narrow question: "What are some of the materials which the Indians used in building their homes?" He might ask the broad question, based on the same information: "How did the Indians decide what to use for materials when they built their homes?"

Situation 9A

Mr. Brooks' sixth grade class was giving social studies reports, and as each child finished, the class spent some time talking about the report.

"How many of you liked that report?" asked Mr. Brooks when James had finished. "What did you think was good about it, Nan?"

"Well, I thought it was interesting, and I liked the way he gave it."

"Anyone else have a comment?" inquired Mr. Brooks. "Yvonne."

"I think he could have spoken louder."

"All right. Anyone else? No. Then would you please be next, Susan?"

When Susan had completed her report, Mr. Brooks said, "Thank you, Susan. How many of you liked Susan's report? Barry, what did you like about it?"

"I thought it was a good report. I think she put a lot of work into it."

"Anyone else? Blake."

"I thought she made it interesting."

"John."

"I think she might have had more about the industries."

"Anyone else? Then who would like to be next? Nan."

Mr. Brooks thanked Nan when she had finished, and asked, "Who has something to say to Nan? Frank?"

"I think hers could have been more interesting, although parts were good."

"Janet."

"Well, I liked hers. I thought it was very good."

"Connie."

"Sometimes she could have looked out at the class more and not always read it."

"All right. Anyone else have anything to say to Nan? Then I think we've had enough reports for today. We'll carry on with them tomorrow, and we'll continue to help each other with our comments after each report."

ANALYSIS   Although this teacher asks the pupils to comment on the reports of their classmates, their comments do not provide much helpful feedback. The teacher does nothing to build upon what the pupils say.

What do you think of the teacher's practice of thanking pupils for their classroom contributions? What does this say about the role of the teacher in that classroom?

SKILL SESSION   Take each pupil comment in this situation and expand it so that it gives helpful feedback without being negative.

Situation 9B

Mr. Plesser's sixth grade class was giving social studies reports, and as each student finished, the class discussed his work.

"Do we have anything to say that might help us as we continue giving reports?" asked Mr. Plesser, when the first youngster had completed her report. "Jack."

"It was a good report—kept me interested all the way through."

"What made it interesting?" probed Mr. Plesser. "Remember what we said about general comments like 'good, interesting, dull, needs more work'? We can be more helpful if we're more specific. We need to think about the 'whys'. Jack, just why did you remain interested?"

"Well, her voice was good. She didn't just read it. She talked."

"And you could tell it wasn't just copied," Anna joined in. "She made it interesting because when she talked about the growth of their big cities, she compared that to what we had talked about in class in our other units."

"So some of the reasons why Vera's report was interesting were that she talked to us and didn't just read her report, and she brought in things that she knew we had discussed before and were interested in. And did you notice also," asked Mr. Plesser, "that she looked about at all of us, and not just down at the table or only at one or two people? Any other comments?"

When no one in the class spoke, Mr. Plesser continued, "What did you think of her use of charts?"

"They were good. I mean they were well made, and you could see them easily."

"Did they help Vera make the points she was trying to make?" Mr. Plesser inquired. "Did they add something, or would it have been just as easy to understand what she meant without the charts?"

"I think they helped. Because if somebody just reads that part it's boring and you don't pay attention. But this way you can look while she talks, so it's better."

"I think these comments will help all of us with our reports," declared Mr. Plesser. "Now, who would like to be next? Milt."

When Milt had completed his report, Mr. Plesser spoke again. "Who has some comments? Claire?"

"I didn't think Milt's was as good as Vera's—not as interesting, and he didn't have any charts."

"Mr. Plesser said we wouldn't compare each other's reports. We're supposed to think about each one alone."

"Yes," agreed Mr. Plesser. "I think Claire forgot about that. Remember, our comments are designed to help the *person* who gave the report as well as the rest of us, which means that negative comments have to be given carefully, in ways that will help, not hurt. We need to include suggestions for improvement, in a way that's really helpful."

"Well, you don't always have to have charts," Milt spoke up. "And I didn't see any place where charts would help me."

"You could have had some when you talked about the different industries," responded Claire. "Then we'd remember them better."

"That's more specific, Claire. You might have said originally that a chart could have helped us to see the importance of the various industries more clearly. It is true," continued Mr. Plesser, "that charts are not essential to every report. We have to make the decision about whether or not to have charts after thinking about what they will add to our reports. Are there other comments?"

"He could have made parts of it shorter—like the part about the number of people who work in each industry. We won't remember that anyway."

"Let's spend a moment on that comment. I think it's probably true," noted Mr. Plesser, "that we won't remember things such as the number of people who work in an industry, even if we see those numbers on a chart. Why not?"

"Because you can't remember long lists of numbers."

"Is it important to know which industries employ more people?" inquired Mr. Plesser.

"Yes."

"Why?"

"Well, so you know what most people in the country do. Are they farmers or what?"

"Milt, how could you give this information in your report without using the exact numbers?" Mr. Plesser questioned.

"You could tell which industry had the most people, and next most, and so on," responded Milt.

"Do you think you could use percentages here?" asked Mr. Plesser.

"Yes—that would be good," said Milt.

"So here's a chance for us to use percentages," said Mr. Plesser. "In math tomorrow let's take Milt's figures and put them into percentages—it will be good practice for us, and this will give us another tool to use in some reports."

ANALYSIS Compare the interaction in this situation with that in situation 9A. Note that situation 9B has more extended talk on the part of both teacher and pupils, and that the teacher does not speak after each pupil speaks.

What effects do you think these different approaches to pupil evaluation in situations 9A and 9B will have on the students and their work?

Why is it that pupils so often evaluate each other's work negatively unless helped to do otherwise by the teacher?

SKILL SESSION Often when teachers evaluate the work of students they begin by being positive, and then add a "but." Remove the "buts" from the following statements (hence, remove the rejection) yet say essentially the same thing. For instance, "I thought your report had an informative summary, but you might have given us more information about what a typical day was like for children," might be said, "I thought your report had an informative summary. Were you able to find any information on what a typical day was like for children?"

1. You read the words without error, but your reading could be more interesting.

2. The picture is quite good, but you might have made the trees larger.

3. You have gone through the proper processes, but your answer is wrong because of an error in addition.

4. Your singing is good, but it isn't loud enough.

5. You told the story well, but can you look at the audience when you speak?

6. You were very quiet as we came down the hall, but when we came to the room you should have gone straight to your seats.

7. Your tests were good on the whole, but I think you could have done even better.

Situation 10

Mrs. James was telling her seventh grade class what she thought of their behavior in the halls. "I was never so ashamed in my life. Everyone was looking at you because you were so noisy. If I've told you once I've told you a hundred times that we are to walk through the halls quietly. I will *not* have you disturbing other classes and other teachers. What *is* the matter with you? Why can't you behave? Is there any excuse for your behavior?"

When no response came from the class, Mrs. James continued, "You have nothing to say because there *are* no excuses for your behavior. Now, if you make noise like that in the halls again, you are going to be sorry. You can't act like first graders and expect to be treated like seventh graders!"

ANALYSIS Using the VICS, categorize these three teacher statements from this situation: "What *is* the matter with you? Why can't you behave? Is there any excuse for your behavior?"

The teacher in this situation uses extended rejecting talk—rejecting the behavior of the pupils in the halls. "I was never so ashamed in my life," is an example of a teacher statement designed to make pupils feel guilty because they have made the teacher unhappy. Teachers do feel the pressure of other adults in their schools about the work and behavior of pupils, and their feelings can be discussed with children. However, it is probably better to talk with youngsters about such things in a way that is less accusative and more informative.

Certainly, teachers can let pupils know of their feelings, and can do so in a forthright manner. A teacher might say, "I felt ashamed when this class made so much noise in the hall," or "I become upset when pupils are cruel to each other," or "Fighting in the school yard makes me terribly angry." These latter statements are less likely to make pupils defensive than the statements made by the teacher in this case, and therefore students will be more likely to listen and evaluate their behavior objectively. The kind of rejecting statements found in situation 10 are often not effective in changing pupil behavior.

SKILL SESSION   Role play a situation in which the pupils have been noisy going through the halls. The teacher will tell the class of his feelings, but in a less accusing manner than the teacher in situation 10. The teacher should encourage the pupils to speak.

Situation 11

Mr. Flack had decided to ask his eighth graders to mark themselves in science, and he was discussing this with them.

"I will still retain the right to change your grade if I disagree, but I'll not do this unless I have a conference with you first. Before I ask you to go ahead with your own evaluation, I thought we'd do a few together, using some sample descriptions, which I have written, of make-believe students. After I finish, you write down a grade, and then we'll discuss the grades we've given. Are you ready? This first student—let's say his name is Ned—did very well in all of his tests, always getting As. He didn't always hand in his homework on time, and his written work was kind of messy. If he was interested in the topic, he participated in class discussion, but a lot of the time he read or sketched in his notebook. His project for the science fair won first prize. That's it—now, put down the grade you would give to Ned, and then we'll talk."

When the youngsters had had a moment to note the grade they would give, Mr. Flack asked, "How many gave him A? Six of you. And how many gave B? Twelve. C? Six. And how many of you gave Ned D? Two people. Now, those of you who gave A—why did you?"

"Because he was a good student, and he did A work."

"You said he got A in all his tests and that's what should count."

"And his science project got first prize. He's good in science, and the mark should tell about how he does in science."

"Any of the others of you give As for other reasons? All right then," Mr. Flack went on, "some of you who gave B. What were your reasons?"

"Well, I gave B because even if he got A in tests, he didn't always talk in class, and he didn't hand in his homework on time. So he doesn't deserve A."

"And his work was messy, and he didn't always pay attention."

"If you give him A, he won't improve his other things—like handing his work in on time. So I gave him B."

"What about the people who gave C's. What reasons did you have?" inquired Mr. Flack.

"I gave him C because he doesn't pay attention in class, and he doesn't hand his work in."

"And he wastes his time and doesn't pay attention. And his work isn't neat."

"He shouldn't get A or B because those are good marks, and then he won't ever improve. So I gave him C."

"All right—what about the D people?" continued Mr. Flack. "A couple of you give D's."

"I gave him a D because that's all he deserves. Just because he did well on tests and got a first prize doesn't mean he should get a good mark. He doesn't work hard; he loafs."

"And he doesn't do some of his work, and he doesn't even pay attention. He draws."

"Well, we see a great difference here, don't we? All the way from A to D, and yet we all heard the same facts about Ned. Why is that?" asked Mr. Flack.

"Some kids mark for some things, and other kids mark for other things."

"Some of us gave the mark on the tests and on how good he was in science—how much he knew. And some kids marked on other things."

"What other things?" probed Mr. Flack.

"Well—did he pay attention, did he pass his work in on time, was he neat—things like that."

"Is there some way we could have more agreement on the grades?" wondered Mr. Flack.

"We can't have more agreement, because we think different things are important."

"Well we might say *how* we are going to decide."

"Yeah, if we made some rules first, then we could agree more."

"All right. We could set up some rules for ourselves, some criteria, and then we might have more agreement. Right now," Mr. Flack went on, "I don't want to spend the time that it would take for us to agree on these rules, so suppose *I* decide that we will grade *only* on academic performance—only on how well the students do on tests, how much science they really know, and so forth. Nothing else. Let's see what happens. Here are the facts about the second student. Grace was the oldest child in a very poor family, and she had to help with housework and help take care of the other children, because her mother went out to work when she came home from school and didn't return until eleven at night. Grace tried very hard, but often didn't have time to do her homework, and she was usually tired during the day and had trouble concentrating. Her class participation was poor and her test grades were never higher than D. All right, now give your grade."

After a short interval, Mr. Flack asked, "How many of you marked Grace A? None. How many gave B? None. C? None. D? Everyone. Reasons?"

"I don't think it's fair, but I gave D."

"We *had* to mark on how good she was in science, so she got D. But it's not fair."

"What *is* fair?" inquired Mr. Flack.

"It shouldn't be just how much you know, because some kids try and some don't and that should be in the grade."

"And some might be doing their best, and they improve, but they might only do C work, and other kids might do their worst work, and not even try, and do B work, or even A. So it wouldn't be fair."

"When I was in elementary school we had two marks—one for effort, and one for achievement. That would be better."

"I agree that that would be better," agreed Mr. Flack. "And I think that some written comments from the teacher would probably be even better, as well as conferences with parents and students. But, in the meantime, we have only one grade in this school, and so I have to put A, B, C, or D on your report cards. In this school we put the main emphasis on academic achievement, but we do take other things into consideration. Now, I want you to write a paragraph or two on your work, telling why you have given yourself a

particular grade. But first, let's make a list of things we want to consider when we grade, and then we'll discuss how much importance we
should give to the various things we decide on. What shall we consider
when we grade?"

"Tests."

"Homework."

"If you talk in the discussions."

"I think we should count. . . ."

ANALYSIS   Analyze the interaction in this situation by referring to
the VICS categories.

Discuss this teacher's assumptions about the
place of evaluation in teaching.

What might be some of the things these
children will learn from this activity?

SKILL SESSION   Divide into groups of five or six, with one of the
group being the observer, and discuss the place of grading and report
cards in education. The observer will note the interaction. After about
ten or fifteen minutes of discussion, talk about the kind of interaction
which occurred in your group.

Situation 12

Mrs. Henry was speaking to one of her
eighth graders about the work he had been doing in English. "For this
marking period your work so far adds up to a D. However, it seems to
me that you aren't working up to your capacity, Ben. What do you
think?"

"I don't know. I guess English isn't my best subject."

"What is your best subject?"

"Well, I like math and sciences most. I want to be a scientist."

"That certainly would be a good choice for you. I know your
grades there are excellent. But, you know, in order to get into college, so that you can become a scientist, you're going to have to
do much better in English. No matter what field you choose, your
writing ability will be considered, and your ability to use the English language. Now, look at this paper. You've mispelled about ten
words, your writing is practically illegible and your thoughts don't
seem to run in any kind of sequence. You jump from one idea to

another without fully developing anything. And you start a new paragraph where none is needed, but when you begin a new topic, much of the time you don't even bother with a new paragraph."

"I just can't seem to write well. And I never could spell," said Ben.

"You say that almost proudly," commented Mrs. Henry. "But really, Ben, you're going to have to put some real effort into your work in this subject from now on. At the rate you're going you won't be able to write up the results of any scientific work you do so that anyone will understand what you've done. If you can get A's in math and science you can certainly do better work in English. I'm willing to help you, but you'll have to cooperate. Now, what do you say?"

"Well, I guess I can try. But I'm not sure if I'll ever be any good in English," replied Ben.

"Well, all I ask is that you be willing to try. I'm going to expect some real improvement from you—and that means no more papers like this one!" concluded Mrs. Henry.

ANALYSIS Describe the interaction in this situation by using the VICS categories.

It is a truism that different pupils react differently to the same teacher statements. Do you think that this pupil will be helped to improve his work by this talk, or will he be discouraged—and why? How does the age and past experience of a student affect the way he reacts to evaluation?

SKILL SESSION Divide into groups of two or three (with the third person being the observer) and role play this kind of evaluation conference, in which a teacher discusses the poor work of an individual student. Assign different characteristics to the student (shy, brash, low ability, and so forth) and change the teacher talk accordingly. Decide on the age of the pupil beforehand.

Situation 13

Mr. Allen decided to have his ninth grade math class evaluate the utility of their year's work now that that year was drawing to a close.

"We've just about finished our algebra course, boys and girls, and I thought we'd spend some time thinking back over what we've learned. How do you think this year's work will help you in the future?"

"Well, we need this course for the advanced algebra course, and also it will help us in college math."

"Right. This course will help you in *any* other math course that you'll be taking, either here or in college. Other ways that this course will help you?"

"My brother's studying to be an engineer, and he said you really have to know math to be an engineer."

"That's very true. I think quite a few of you are interested in becoming engineers, and algebra will certainly be essential to you as you go on. Anything else?"

"Well, I want to be a kindergarten teacher, and I really can't see how algebra is going to help me."

"And I don't even want to go to college. I'm not going to take any more math, and I don't see how algebra is going to help me any."

"Don't you remember that we said a knowledge of algebra and its principles is important in almost every aspect of life? And certainly you want to be an educated person. You'll be surprised at how much your algebra will mean to you, no matter what you do in the future. Now, let's think a little harder about just how we'll be helped by this year's work."

"I might be a scientist, and I guess algebra will help me with that."

"Exactly. You're really thinking. Anyone else like to tell us how algebra will help us in our future lives?"

ANALYSIS   What is the teacher in this situation really interested in accomplishing in this session? What do you thnk the pupils will learn as a result?

SKILL SESSION   Role play this situation, but have the teacher accept all pupil contributions. The teacher should summarize the results of the discussion at the conclusion of the evaluation session.

CHAPTER 10

The Improvement
of Teaching

ASSUMPTIONS
ABOUT THE IMPROVEMENT
OF TEACHING

Several assumptions about improving teaching are fundamental to the point of view and the method of presentation in this book. The assumptions are that teaching can be subjected to systematic inquiry, that teaching involves behavior which can be identified and acquired, and that teachers and prospective teachers want to improve their teaching behavior.

1. *Teaching can be submitted to systematic inquiry* Teaching takes place in classrooms and involves human beings in group situations. Observational procedures can be applied to the classroom group just as they can be applied to any human group which involves interaction. Because of its relatively predictable and long-term existence, the classroom group actually lends itself to intensive study more easily than many other groups that social scientists have thoroughly analyzed. When human beings interact with each other, this interaction can be observed, analyzed, studied, and predicted.

2. *Teaching involves behaviors which can be identified, and which teachers and prospective teachers can systematically acquire* If teaching is to be improved, then these behaviors must be looked at neither as a mysterious set of indefinable traits which are inborn, nor as capabilities which automatically accrue to college graduates who know their subject matter. Rather, these behaviors should be regarded as skills which can be consciously acquired through the study and analysis of classroom interaction, and which can be practiced and controlled in and out of the classroom.

3. *Teachers and prospective teachers want to improve their teaching*
Given the necessary help and encouragement, human beings want to
grow and develop, and teachers, whose work has particular importance
for society and for its individual members, may have a particularly
strong drive to improve their skills.

CONDITIONS IMPORTANT
FOR THE IMPROVEMENT
OF TEACHING

Certain conditions appear to be important
for the improvement of teaching. These conditions are the desire for
change, a climate of support, a system which can be used for studying
teaching and providing feedback, and an opportunity to practice new
teaching behaviors.

1. *A desire for change is important if teaching is to be improved.*
Since teachers and prospective teachers want to improve their teaching
according to the third assumption stated above, then this condition
for the improvement of teaching is present, although it clearly is not
always capitalized upon. To say that the desire for change is important
in order for teaching to be improved is not the same as saying that the
initiative for change must emanate from teachers. The initiative and
the ideas may come from other sources, in or out of the profession, but
teachers must be involved to the extent that they want to participate,
if growth and development are to occur.

2. *A climate of support is important for the improvement of teaching* This climate should come primarily from supervisory personnel
and fellow teachers, but support can also be obtained from other
sources such as professional education courses, books or journals, and
workshops or meetings. For undergraduate students, the support would
come from such sources as college teachers, cooperating teachers, and
fellow students. Rarely can a person find enough support within himself to initiate and carry through a systematic program of improvement.
It is the presence or absence of a climate of support which determines
whether or not the desire for change present in teachers and future
teachers will be capitalized upon.

3. *A system which objectively describes what occurs in the classroom
and can be used for feedback is important to the improvement of teach-*

ing Such a system is useful for describing teaching so that this phenomenon may be studied and analyzed, and it also is helpful for providing teachers and prospective teachers with objective data about their own behavior. The use of an objective system which describes classroom interaction helps students and teachers to understand that scientific method can be applied to the study of teaching. When the system is used as a feedback tool, those using it can be provided with information about their own behavior in a way which allows them to retain and develop what they want to keep, and eliminate or modify those behaviors with which they are not satisfied.

4. *An opportunity to practice new teaching behaviors is important to the improvement of teaching* The opportunity to practice can be provided through the use of skill sessions in college classes or in workshops, or directly in the classroom with pupils. Through practice, new behaviors can be internalized and thus produced spontaneously in appropriate situations.

THE ROLE
AND LIMITATIONS
OF THIS BOOK

Although this book might be of some help in providing the climate of support necessary to capitalize on the desire of teachers and future teachers to improve their teaching, its major strengths are related to the third and fourth conditions listed above as being important for the improvement of teaching: the usefulness of a system which described classroom interaction and which could be used for feedback; and the need for an opportunity to practice new teaching behaviors. Throughout this book the Verbal Interaction Category System has been presented as a system which can be used by teachers and those preparing to be teachers to study and analyze teaching, and also as a feedback tool. The situations in the book and the analyses that follow were presented to meet the third condition listed as being important to improved teaching. The skill sessions were designed to meet the fourth condition, by encouraging the practice of new teaching behaviors. The book as a whole was written so that those who read it and participate in the activities presented will become better teachers—teachers who are capable of analyzing and controlling their verbal behavior, teachers who have a broader repertoire of verbal behaviors from which to select; thus, teachers who are better able to help children learn.

Selected References

Amidon, Edmund, "Interaction Analysis and Its Application to Student Teaching," *Theoretical Bases for Professional Laboratory Experiences in Teacher Education*, 44th Yearbook. The Association for Student Teaching. Cedar Falls, Iowa: State College of Iowa, 1965.

Amidon, Edmund, and Ned A. Flanders, *The Role of the Teacher in the Classroom*. Minneapolis: Paul S. Amidon and Associates, 1963.

Amidon, Edmund, and Anita Simon, "Teacher-Pupil Interaction," *Review of Educational Research*, vol. 35, no. 2 (April, 1965).

Bellack, Arno A., and others, *The Language of the Classroom: Meanings Communicated in High School Teaching*. U.S. Department of Health, Education, and Welfare, Office of Education, Cooperative Research Project no. 1497. New York: Institute of Psychological Research, Columbia University, 1963.

Biddle, Bruce J., and William J. Elena, eds., *Contemporary Research on Teacher Effectiveness*. New York: Holt, Rinehart and Winston, Inc., 1964.

Bowers, Norman D., and Robert S. Soar, *Studies of Human Relations in the Teaching-Learning Process. V. Final Report: Evaluation of Laboratory Human Relations Training for Classroom Teachers*. U.S. Department of Health, Education, and Welfare, Office of Education, Cooperative Research Project no. 469. Chapel Hill, N.C.: University of North Carolina, 1961.

Dewey, John, "The Relation of Theory to Practice in Education," *National Society for the Scientific Study of Education*, Third Yearbook (1904). Reprinted by the Association for Student Teaching, Bull. 17 (1962). Cedar Falls, Iowa: State College of Iowa, p. 7.

Dewey, John, "The Sources of a Science of Education," *Kappa Delta Pi Lecture Series.* New York: Liveright Publishing Corporation, 1929, p. 10.

Flanders, Ned A., *Teacher Influence, Pupil Attitudes, and Achievement.* Cooperative Research Monograph no. 12, U.S. Department of Health, Education, and Welfare, Office of Education. Washington, D.C.: U.S. Government Printing Office, 1965.

Gage, N. L., ed., *Handbook of Research on Teaching.* Skokie, Ill.: Rand McNally & Company, 1963, p. 91.

Gallagher, James J., and Mary Jane M. Aschner, "A Preliminary Report: Analyses of Classroom Interaction," *Merrill-Palmer Quarterly of Behavior and Development,* vol. 9 (July, 1963), pp. 183–194.

HDI Program, *General Relationship Improvement Program,* 4th ed. Atlanta, Georgia: Human Development Institute, Inc., 1964.

Hughes, Marie M., "Utah Study of the Assessment of Teaching," *Theory and Research in Teaching,* Arno A. Bellack, ed. New York. Columbia University, Teachers College, Bureau of Publications, 1963, pp. 25–36.

Hughes, Marie M., "What Is Teaching? One Viewpoint," *Educational Leadership,* vol. 19, no. 4 (January, 1962).

Hunter, Elizabeth, and Edmund Amidon, *Student Teaching: Cases and Comments.* New York: Holt, Rinehart and Winston, Inc., 1964.

Medley, Donald M., and Harold E. Mitzel, "Measuring Classroom Behavior by Systematic Observation," *Handbook of Research on Teaching,* N. L. Gage, ed. Skokie, Ill.: Rand McNally & Company, 1963, pp. 247–328.

Medley, Donald M., "Experiences with the OSCAR Technique," *Professional Reprints in Education* no. 8606. Columbus, Ohio: Charles E. Merrill Books, Inc., 1965.

Nichols, Hildred, and Lois Williams, *Learning about Role-Playing for Children and Teachers.* Bull. no. 66, Association for Childhood Education International, Washington, D.C., 1960.

Raths, Louis, "What Is a Good Teacher?" *Professional Reprints in Education* no. 8602. Columbus, Ohio: Charles E. Merrill Books, Inc., 1965.

Sarasan, Seymour B., Kenneth S. Davidson, and Burton Blatt, *The Preparation of Teachers: An Unstudied Problem in Education.* New York: John Wiley & Sons, Inc., 1962.

Smith, B. Othanel, "A Conceptual Analysis of Instructional Behavior,"

Professional Reprints in Education no. 8604. Columbus, Ohio: Charles E. Merrill Books, Inc., 1965.

Smith, B. Othanel, and R. H. Ennis, eds., *Language and Concepts in Education*. Skokie, Ill.: Rand McNally & Company, 1961.

Suchman, J. Richard, "Inquiry Training: Building Skills for Autonomous Discovery," *Merrill-Palmer Quarterly*, vol. 7 (July, 1961), pp. 147–169.

Sullivan, George, *The Image of the Effective Teacher*. New York: The Central School Study, Teachers College, Columbia University, 1963.

Symonds, Percival, *What Education Has to Learn from Psychology*. New York: Bureau of Publications, Teachers College, Columbia University, 1958.

Taba, Hilda, and others, *Thinking in Elementary School Children*. U.S. Department of Health, Education, and Welfare, Office of Education, Cooperative Research Project no. 1574. San Francisco: San Francisco State College, 1964.

Taba, Hilda, and Freeman F. Elzey, "Teaching Strategies and Thought Processes," *Professional Reprints in Education* no. 8603. Columbus, Ohio: Charles E. Merrill Books, Inc. 1965.

Taba, Hilda, and James L. Hills, *Teacher Handbook for Contracosta Social Studies Grades 1–6*. Hayward, Cal.: Rapid Printers and Lithographers, Inc., 1965.

Withall, John, and W. W. Lewis, "Social Interaction in the Classroom," *Handbook of Research on Teaching*, N. L. Gage, ed. Skokie, Ill.: Rand McNally & Company, 1963.

The Verbal Interaction Category System (VICS)

The Verbal Interaction Category System is based upon the Flanders system of Interaction Analysis, and contains five major categories for analyzing classroom verbal behavior. They are: teacher-initiated talk, teacher response, pupil response, pupil initiated talk, and other. Table I summarizes the categories in the Flanders system and Table II indicates those in the VICS.

Both of these systems require that persons planning to use them in order to study verbal behavior in the classroom begin by memorizing the categories. Once these are learned so that response is automatic, tapes of various teaching situations should be used for practicing the tallying of categories. A category is tallied every three seconds, in sequence, in a column, indicating the interaction which is occurring at the time. If the verbal behavior changes before the three-second interval ends, this change is always recorded. Approximately twenty numbers are written per minute. Ultimately, in the VICS, the categories are entered in a seventeen-row by seventeen-column table called a matrix, which presents information clearly and succinctly about the type, sequence, and amount of verbal behavior which has occurred.

THE VICS CATEGORIES

Teacher-Initiated Talk

1. *Gives Information or Opinion* This category is tallied when the teacher is presenting facts or opinions to the class, either in the form of short statements or in the form of extended lecture. Generally, when the teacher is presenting content, this category is being used. Explanation and orientation would fall in this category. During the interchange of discussion a teacher often gives information or opinion. Rhetorical questions such as, "We wouldn't expect that the government would have ceded power willingly, would we?" are tallied in this category.

Table I

CATEGORIES IN THE FLANDERS SYSTEM OF INTERACTION ANALYSIS

Teacher Talk	*Indirect Influence*	**1.** Accepts Feeling: accepts and clarifies the feeling tone of the students in a nonthreatening manner. Feelings may be positive or negative. Predicting or recalling feelings are included.
		2. Praises or Encourages: praises or encourages student action or behavior. Jokes that release tension, not at the expense of another individual, nodding head or saying "um hm?" or "go on" are included.
		3. Accepts or Uses Ideas of Student: clarifying, building, or developing ideas or suggestions by a student. As teacher brings more of his own ideas into play, shift to category five.
		4. Asks Questions: asking a question about content or procedure with the intent that a student answer.
	Direct Influence	**5.** Lecturing: giving facts or opinions about content or procedure: Expressing his own ideas, asking rhetorical questions.
		6. Giving Directions: directions, commands, or orders which a student is expected to comply with.
		7. Criticizing or Justifying Authority: statements intended to change student behavior from nonacceptable to acceptable pattern; bawling someone out; stating why the teacher is doing what he is doing; extreme self-reference.
Student Talk		**8.** Student Talk-Response: talk by student in response to teacher. Teacher initiates the contact or solicits student statement.
		9. Student Talk-Initiation: talk by students which they initiate. If "calling on" student is only way to indicate who may talk next, observer must decide whether student wanted to talk. If he did, use this category.
		10. Silence or Confusion: pauses, short periods of silence and periods of confusion in which communication cannot be understood by the observer.

Table II

THE VERBAL INTERACTION CATEGORY SYSTEM (VICS)

Teacher-Initiated Talk	**1.** Gives Information or Opinion: presents content or own ideas, explains, orients, asks rhetorical questions. May be short statements or extended lecture.
	2. Gives Direction: tells pupil to take some specific action; gives orders; commands.
	3. Asks Narrow Question: asks drill questions, questions requiring one or two word replies or yes-or-no answers; questions to which the specific nature of the response can be predicted.
	4. Asks Broad Question: asks relatively open-ended questions which call for unpredictable responses; questions which are thought-provoking. Apt to elicit a longer response than 3.
Teacher Response	**5.** Accepts: (5a) Ideas: reflects, clarifies, encourages or praises ideas of pupils. Summarizes, or comments without rejection.
	(5b) Behavior: responds in ways which commend or encourage pupil behavior.
	(5c) Feeling: responds in ways which reflect or encourage expression of pupil feeling.
	6. Rejects: (6a) Ideas: criticizes, ignores or discourages pupil ideas.
	(6b) Behavior: discourages or criticizes pupil behavior. Designed to stop undesirable behavior. May be stated in question form, but differentiated from category 3 or 4, and from category 2, Gives Direction, by tone of voice and resultant effect on pupils.
	(6c) Feeling: ignores, discourages, or rejects pupil expression of feeling.
Pupil Response	**7.** Responds (7a) Predictably: relatively short replies, usually, which follow category 3. May also to follow category 2, i.e. "David, you may Teacher: read next."
	(7b) Unpredictably: replies which usually follow category 4.
	8. Responds to Another Pupil: replies occurring in conversation between pupils.
Pupil-Initiated Talk	**9.** Initiates Talk to Teacher: statements which pupils direct to teacher without solicitation from teacher.
	10. Initiates Talk to Another Pupil: statements which pupils direct to another pupil which are not solicited.
Other	**11.** Silence: pauses or short periods of silence during a time of classroom conversation.
	Z. Confusion: considerable noise which disrupts planned activities. This category may accompany other categories or may totally preclude the use of other categories.

4
7b[1]
7b
3
7a[2]
1
2
9[3]
1
4
7b[2]

Numbers may be placed to the right of and slightly above the category numbers to indicate change in pupils who are participating:

---

2. *Gives Directions* When the teacher tells the students to take some specific action, this category is used. Examples of category 2 are: "Open your books to page 5," "Take your seats now," and "Add the following numbers as quickly as possible." Directions may be given in question form, as for example, "Will everyone turn around now?" or "Can you come here for a moment, Jane?"

3. *Asks Narrow Question* If the specific nature of the response can be predicted, then this category is tallied. Drill questions and questions requiring one word or yes-or-no answers fall into this category. "How much is 3 and 3?" "What is the capital of France?" "Is that correct?" "What happened next in the story?" "What are the principal exports of Brazil?" and "Did you like that plan?" are examples of narrow questions.

4. *Asks Broad Question* Questions that fall into this category would be relatively open-ended; the kind that call for unpredictable responses. When the teacher asks questions that are thought-provoking, that require reasoning, or extended expression of opinion or feeling, this category is used. The broad question is apt to elicit longer responses than the narrow question. Examples of broad questions are: "Can you tell me some things you know about the number '3'?" "What are some reasons that Paris came to be the capital of France?" "What are some other things the author might have written next in this story?" "What are some ways in which the history and geography of Brazil might influence its production and exports?" "What do you think about that plan?" and "How do you feel about what she said?"

Teacher Response

5a. *Accepts Ideas* When the teacher clarifies, reflects, encourages, or praises an idea of a pupil, then this category is tallied. If the teacher summarizes the ideas of a pupil or of several pupils, comments upon the ideas without rejecting them or simply reflects them by restatement, this category is indicated. Saying, "Yes," "Good," "That's an interesting idea," and "So you think the governor acted wisely," are examples of category 5a.

5b.   *Accepts Behavior*   Responses to pupil behavior that encourage or praise that behavior fall into this category. Such statements as, "The boys and girls in this group are cooperating well," "Billy knows how to use books properly," "You told that story with marvelous expression," "That's a colorful picture," "You can be proud of the way you behaved on our trip," and "Good work," are examples of acceptance of behavior.

5c.   *Accepts Feeling*   When the teacher responds to pupil feeling in an accepting manner or merely reflects their feelings, this category is tallied. "I know that it's a warm day and many of us would rather be outside," "Of course you feel disappointed because there isn't any assembly program today," "I'd be happy too, if that happened to me," "No wonder you're crying," and "You're very angry," are examples of category 5c.

6a.   *Rejects Ideas*   This category is used when the teacher criticizes, ignores or discourages pupil ideas. "Can someone else tell us the right answer?" "That's not right," "Where did you ever get *that* idea!" "Is that what I asked you to discuss?" and "New York is not one of the New England States," are examples of rejection. Notice that some of these examples were stated in question form, but would be taken by the pupils as criticism, and are clearly rejection of ideas.

6b.   *Rejects Behavior*   Teacher comments that are designed to discourage or criticize pupil behavior fall into this category. "I said to sit down!" "We shouldn't have our books open now," "Where do you think you are?" "Stop that at once," and "Never give me a paper like that again," are all expressions of rejection of behavior. Some of these examples may appear to fall into the category of questions of directions. The tone of voice, the resultant effect upon pupils, and the fact that they are designed to stop behaviors which the teacher considers to be *undesirable* are what cause them to be categorized as teacher comments which reject pupil behavior.

6c.   *Rejects Feeling*   When teachers respond to expressions of pupil feeling by discouraging or criticizing them, then the category of rejecting feeling is being used. "Aren't you ashamed of yourself for crying?" "Just because there's no assembly today is no reason to mope," "There's no need to bring our personal feelings up," and "There's absolutely no reason for you to be worried," are examples of this category.

Pupil Response

7a. *Responds to Teacher Predictably* This response would ordinarily follow category 3, a narrow or predictable response question from the teacher, and would tend to be a relatively short reply. Category 7a may also follow category 2, Giving Direction, as when the teacher says, "David, read the sentence at the top of the page." A response that is incorrect may still be considered to be in this category.

7b. *Responds to Teacher Unpredictably* This category would usually follow the asking of a broad or unpredictable response question by the teacher. However, it is possible for a pupil to give an unpredictable response to a question which is categorized as narrow. For instance, when a teacher asks, "What was the cause of this conflict?" a pupil might reply, "It seems to me that there wasn't any one cause. I think there were many factors at work." This kind of response, however, is rarely found in the classroom. It would be more likely that an unpredictable response to a narrow question would be an irrelevant response, as when the teacher asks, "How many of you had milk for breakfast this morning?" and a pupil responds, "Last night we had ice cream for dessert."

8. *Responds to Another Pupil* Whenever one pupil responds to the question or statement of another pupil, this category is being used. When there is conversation between pupils, the replies are examples of category 8.

Pupil-Initiated Talk

9. *Talks to Teacher* If a pupil initiates a conversation with the teacher, then category 9 is tallied. "Will we have art today?" "I don't understand how to do this problem," "Here's a clipping I brought in for our social studies project," "Would you repeat that last part again," are all examples of category 9.

10. *Talks to Another Pupil* Any conversation which one pupil initiates with another pupil falls into this category.

Other

11. *Silence* Category 11 is tallied when there are pauses or short periods of silence. For long periods of silence, as when the class is engaged in seat work or silent reading, the observer simply notes this in the margin and stops tallying.

Z. *Confusion* When there is considerable noise which disrupts planned activities, this category is used. Z may also be placed along side another category to indicate some accompanying confusion while the teacher and some pupils continue with the scheduled activities. (See Honigman, references at end of appendix.)

THE MATRIX IN THE VICS

The category numbers which have been tallied in columns during the time of recording are later transferred to a matrix (or may be directly transferred if the recorder is highly trained.) A sample matrix is presented in Figure I. Each square on the matrix is referred to as a cell, and these cells may be either of a transitional nature, or may indicate steady state behavior. Steady state cells will have tallies in them only if the verbal behavior lasted longer than three seconds. All other cells are transitional cells representing movement from one category to another.

The recorder transfers the category numbers which have been tallied in the classroom onto the matrix two at a time, thus indicating the general sequence of interaction. The matrix is a seventeen-row by seventeen-column table which has a total of 289 cells. As an example, the tallies for this conversation are entered in the matrix in Figure I:

Teacher	Open your books to page six.	2
Pupil	Which book should we be looking at?	9
Teacher	If you had paid attention, you would know.	6b
Teacher	Now, on page six there is a diagram which shows the relationship between population density and types of occupation. I think this is an excellent diagram for our purposes.	1 1
Teacher	Does anyone have some ideas about why these two factors might be related?	4 4

When the recorder finishes his tallying, he will pair the numbers in the following fashion.

$$
\begin{array}{l}
\phantom{\text{2nd pair } (}2 \\
\text{2nd pair } (\,9\,) \text{ 1st pair} \\
\phantom{\text{4th pair } (}6b \\
\text{4th pair } (\,1\,) \text{ 3rd pair} \\
\phantom{\text{6th pair } (}1 \\
\text{6th pair } (\,1\,) \text{ 5th pair} \\
\phantom{\text{6th pair } (}4 \\
\phantom{\text{6th pair } (}4\,) \text{ } n\text{th pair}
\end{array}
$$

The first pair is 2–9, the second pair is 9–6b, the third pair is 6b–1, and so on. The particular cell in which the tabulation of the pair of

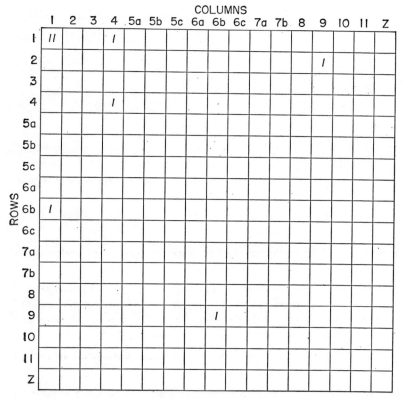

Figure I

numbers is made is determined by using the first number in the pair to indicate the *row,* and second number in the pair to indicate the *column.* Thus, 2–9 would be shown by a tabulation in the cell formed by row 2 and column 9. The second pair, 9–6b, would be shown in the cell formed by row 9 and column 6b. The third pair, 6b–1, is entered in the cell formed by row 6b and column 1. Notice that each pair of numbers overlaps with the previous pair, and each number, except the first and last, is used twice.

Once the tallies are entered on the matrix, then the interaction pattern in the classroom can be interpreted by studying that matrix. Different parts of the matrix indicate different kinds of classroom interaction, as will be seen from Figure II and the following discussion:

AREAS WITHIN THE MATRIX IN THE VICS

Area A   This is the area of prolonged teacher initiation, and includes presenting information or opinion, giving directions and asking questions. The major characteristic of this area is that the teacher is speaking for a relatively long period. This is not an area which shows interaction between pupil and teacher.

Area B   The cells in this area indicate teacher initiated statements followed by teacher response statements, either accepting or rejecting.

Area C   This group of cells includes all pupil talk which follows teacher initiated talk.

Area D   Area D indicates teacher response statements followed by teacher initiated statements.

Area E   This area indicates prolonged accepting behavior on the part of the teacher. This includes extended acceptance of ideas, behavior and feelings, as well as transitions from one of these verbal patterns to another.

Area F   These cells indicate teacher accepting behavior followed by teacher rejecting behavior.

Area G   This area shows accepting teacher statements followed by any student statements.

Area H   Area H indicates teacher rejecting behavior followed by teacher accepting behavior.

Area I   These cells indicate extended rejecting behavior on the part of the teacher. Rejection of ideas, behavior and feelings are indicated here, as well as transition from one of these behaviors to another.

Area J   These cells show all pupil statements which follow teacher rejecting statements.

Area K   This area indicates pupil response behavior followed by teacher initiated behavior.

Area L   This group of cells show student response followed by teacher acceptance.

Area M   Area M shows teacher rejection of pupil responses.

Area N   These cells show extended student response to either the teacher or another pupil.

Area O   Area O indicates pupil response statements followed by pupil initiated statements.

Area P   These cells indicate pupil initiated behavior followed by teacher initiated behavior.

Area Q   This area shows pupil initiated talk followed by teacher acceptance.

Area R   Area R indicates teacher rejection of pupil initiated talk.

Area S   These cells indicate pupil initiated statements followed by student response statements.

Area T   This area indicates extended pupil initiated talk to either the teacher or another pupil.

Area U   Area U indicates silence or confusion. If the tallies are in row or column 11 they indicate silence, and if they are in row or column Z, they indicate confusion. Tallies in column 11 or Z represent silence or confusion following teacher or pupil talk, while tallies in rows 11 or Z represent silence or confusion after pupil or teacher talk.

The matrix indicates the amount, the sequence, and the pattern of verbal behavior in the classroom according

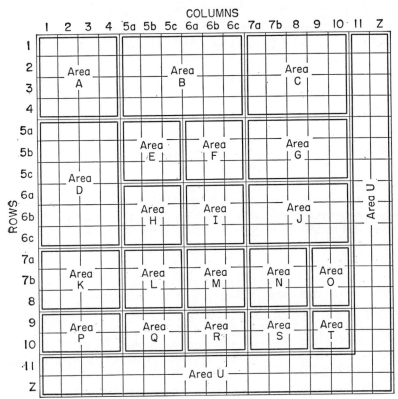

Figure II

to the categories delineated in the VICS. One can determine, for example, how much direction the teacher gave, or how much he accepted or rejected the pupils. One can also determine from the matrix what kind of behavior followed each former behavior. And one can determine recurring patterns in the classroom.

The matrix can indicate, for example, whether or not teacher questions are followed by periods of silence during which students may be thinking about their responses. If a teacher allows pupils time to think before they answer, then the silence category will be followed by a pupil response category, rather than by another teacher category. This is just one example of the wide spectrum of classroom interactive behavior which can be determined from the matrix.

THE IMPLICATIONS
AND POTENTIAL
OF THE VICS FOR
TEACHER EDUCATION

The VICS has particular utility in the field of teacher education. It is a system which can be used to help teachers and student teachers focus upon their behavior in the classroom in an objective manner. By recording their teaching activities on tape, or by having another person trained in the use of the system categorize the verbal behavior in their classrooms, teachers and student teachers may obtain a record of their classroom conversation for analysis. College supervisors of student teaching and cooperating teachers will find that a knowledge of the system is particularly helpful in their work with student teachers.

The use of a system such as this one helps to provide teachers and future teachers with an attitude of inquiry toward the entire area of teaching behavior. They will become conscious of the importance of verbal patterns of which they were not aware before being provided with a system of objective feedback.

It will be seen that the Verbal Interaction Category System for analyzing verbal behavior in the classroom offers teachers, future teachers, and supervisors a tool which can provide objective data about teaching behavior. Objective feedback is a necessary component of teacher growth and change.

REFERENCES

Amidon, E. J., and N. A. Flanders, *The Role of the Teacher in the Classroom.* Minneapolis: Paul Amidon and Associates, 1963.

Anderson, H. H., "The Measurement of Domination and of Socially Integrative Behavior in Teachers' Contact with Children," *Child Development,* vol. 10, no. 2 (1939), pp. 73–79.

Aschner, Mary Jane M., *The Analysis of Classroom Discourse: A Method and its Uses.* Unpublished Doctoral Dissertation, University of Illinois, 1959.

Bales, R. F., *Interaction Process Analysis.* Reading, Mass.: Addison-Wesley Publishing Company, Inc., 1950.

Honigman, R. K., "Synopsis of Innovations and Revisions to the Flanders System of Interaction Analysis." Philadelphia: Temple University, 1964. The procedure for tabulating two categories side by side as a means of recording simultaneously-occurring behaviors was developed by Honigman in 1962. A systematic discussion of this procedure, as well as other innovations and revisions of Interaction Analysis, is presented in this paper.

Hughes, Marie, and others. *Development of the Means for Assessment of the Quality of Teaching in Elementary Schools*. Salt Lake City: University of Utah, 1959.

Medley, D. M., and H. E. Mitzel, "A Technique for Measuring Classroom Behavior," *Journal of Educational Psychology*, vol. 49 (April, 1958), pp. 86–92.

Smith, B. Othanel, "A Concept of Teaching," *Teachers College Record*, vol. 61 (February, 1960), pp. 229–241.

Withall, John, "The Development of a Technique for the Measurement of Social-Emotional Climate in Classrooms," *Journal of Experimental Education*, vol. 17 (March, 1949), pp. 347–361.